Fundamental Analysis for Beginners

Grow Your Investment Portfolio Like A Pro Using Financial Statements and Ratios of Any Business with Zero Investing Experience Required

A.Z Penn

A.Z Penn

Fundamental Analysis for Beginners

A.Z Penn

TABLE OF CONTENTS

HOW TO GET THE MOST OUT OF THIS BOOK...7

Introduction..14

Chapter 1: What is Fundamental Analysis?...18

Chapter 2: Finding Fundamental Data...29

Chapter 3: Beat the Street...49

Chapter 4: The three types of statements you need to know, and where to find them.60

Chapter 5: Why adding two and two sometimes makes more than four..................89

Chapter 6: Industry fundamentals...137

Chapter 7: What CEOs say - and what they mean.............................148

Chapter 8: What's the price tag?..156

Chapter 9: 50 cents now or 10 bucks later?.......................................170

Chapter 10: Macro vs Micro, or Top Down vs Bottom Up................194

Chapter 11: Defining 'buy' and 'sell'..205

Chapter 12: The best of both worlds - combining FA and TA............215

Chapter 13: Top tips...227

Chapter 14: Build a portfolio...238

Conclusion..251

Glossary..260

Quiz Answers..269

TABLE OF CONTENTS

HOW TO GET THE MOST OUT OF THIS BOOK

To help you along your investing journey, I've created two free bonus companion masterclasses, one which includes walking you through an investors mindset on how to find potential companies to invest in. There's also a free companion DCF model spreadsheet of Amazon which I created specifically to simplify your learning of this valuation model. I also provide an additional colored images resource that will help you get the best possible result.

I highly recommend you sign up now to get the most out of this book. You can do that by visiting the link or scanning the QR code below:

www.az-penn.com

Free bonus #1: **Company Valuation Simplified Masterclass ($97 value)**

In this video masterclass, I will be walking you through an investors mindset on how to find potential companies to invest in, which includes what to look out for and major red flags to keep in mind. This class will help you decide whether a company is worth investing in or whether you should move on.

Free bonus #2: **Charting Simplified Masterclass ($67 value)**

In this 5 part video masterclass you'll be discovering various simple and easy to use strategies on making profitable trades. By showing you real life stock examples of a few charting indicators - you will be able to determine whether a stock is worth trading or not.

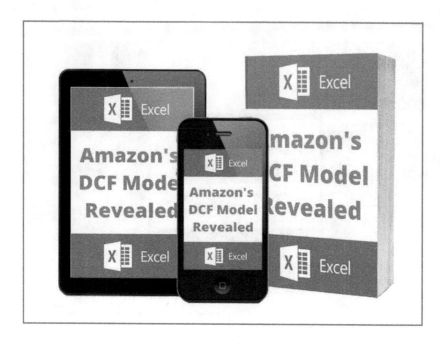

 Amazons DCF Model Revealed ($37 value)

This Excel spreadsheet will be a great companion for you whilst reading this book. It will reveal the complete DCF model calculations I've presented in the book for Amazon. With this insightful spreadsheet, you will find it easier to duplicate my DCF model example on any company you're researching.

Free bonus #4: **Colored Images – Fundamental Analysis for Beginners**

To keep our books at a reasonable price for you, we print in black & white. But here are all the images in full color.

All of these bonuses are 100% free, with no strings attached. You don't need to provide any personal details except your email address.

To get your bonuses, go to the link or QR code:

www.az-penn.com

Fundamental Analysis for Beginners

Introduction

You might think investing in the stock market isn't for you. Or maybe you got started on Robinhood or another trading platform, and you started losing money. That can leave a nasty taste.

But you know something? Investing in the stock market is for everyone!

First of all, if you don't invest in stocks, you're losing out. Over the years, stocks have almost always beaten 'safer' investments like bonds. They give greater annual returns, and over time, the effect of compounding will make a stock based (investment) portfolio vastly outperform a cash and bonds (savings) portfolio. So even if you invest via mutual funds or through ETFs (exchange-traded fund), it's worth investing in the stock market.

For some investors, ETFs are all they want - a relatively trouble-free way to invest. They give you a broad exposure at a low cost. But you'll only do as well as the market as a whole. If the market goes up, the ETF will follow. If it goes down... you get the message. Over time, if you 'buy and hold' forever, you should make a reasonable return (the S&P 500 made an annual return of 10.5% from when it started in 1957, to 2021).

Other investors prefer to pick mutual funds that are more actively managed (a pool of money managed by a professional fund manager). But of course, there's a cost for that management, which will be taken out of your returns. And you don't have a guarantee of beating the market, though some funds have better success than others.

Would you like to improve your return even more? Then direct investment could be the way forward. But if you're going to make it work, you'll need to learn the basic skills of fundamental analysis (which can be more fun than it sounds).

With this, you can ensure that you are investing:

- in companies that have a good, strong business,
- in companies that don't have financial problems waiting to trip them up, and
- in stocks that aren't so highly valued you'll never make money out of them.

Remember that the broader stock market, and consequently the ETFs, come with the rough as well as the smooth. The S&P 500 included the fraudulent, and eventually bankrupted company, Enron - but if you'd looked at Enron's annual report, you'd probably have seen a few issues which might have kept you from investing in the shares in the first place.

So, what is fundamental analysis? In general, it's about understanding each company's business, finance, and value, just as if you were buying the business and not the stock. Fundamental analysis says that the value of a stock is based on what the company actually does, earns, and possesses - and that whatever the market does is just noise. The market goes up and down, but if you've made the right investment at the right price, that shouldn't matter. It can be a worry, but in the long term you should win out.

One big part of fundamental analysis is understanding how the business operates in 'the real world'. For instance, if you're investing in a retail business, you'll need to get a feel for how many stores it's opening, what its footprint is, and what people think about the retailer and its product. But of course, as stock market investors, we're interested in how that comes through to the bottom line - and that's where the numbers come in.

If you read some analyst research, it's easy to think that this is too hard to do or that you need to be a CFA (chartered financial analyst). Remember, professional analysts write for fund managers and other specialists, so they don't have to try to make their reports readable for a non-specialist. They'll even fight battles over the best ratios to use and how to calculate them - but then they're paid for that.

Fundamental Analysis for Beginners

You can use some really basic ratios to assess the strength and health of a company, and it doesn't take a lot of time to learn. In fact, it's not calculating the ratios but understanding the answers that are the most important factor in making good investments.

So, if you didn't excel at math, think accountancy is boring, or don't have 'a head for numbers', it doesn't matter - as long as you can use a spreadsheet and calculate percentages, you can learn to invest wisely and productively. And that's what I'm going to teach you here.

I've traded the stock markets for a while and learned my lessons the hard way. I've made a few mistakes and learned from each one, working out where I had gone wrong. Quite often, I found I had overlooked a warning sign I should have seen in a company's Annual Report, or not noticed that the trends in the company's business were changing. That led me to some very dry reading such as Security Analysis by Graham & Dodd. But the knowledge I gained helped me improve my investment returns significantly.

I still think the books I read were great, but I can't call them user-friendly. That's why I've written *Fundamental Analysis for Beginners*. I want you to learn fundamental analysis easily, without being bored, and with some good real-world examples. If you've made a few mistakes of your own, maybe you'll see where you went wrong and how you can avoid making the same mistake twice. And I hope that by the end of the book, you'll feel confident in your ability to choose the right investments, click your broker's 'buy' button, and start making your money work a bit harder for you than sitting around in a bank account.

Let's get started!

A.Z Penn

1

Chapter 1: What is Fundamental Analysis?

What Fundamental Analysis Isn't

"My friend gave me this great tip" is not fundamental analysis.

"It's trending on Reddit" is not fundamental analysis.

"Warren Buffett bought it" is not fundamental analysis.

"Goldman Sachs' analyst recommended it" is not fundamental analysis.

"I saw it on CNBC" is not fundamental analysis.

"I'm buying because the price is going up" is not fundamental analysis.

"I bought it because it had dipped 10% in an uptrend" is not fundamental analysis.

"It's growing really fast" is not fundamental analysis.

"It's a game-changing technology, and it will control the whole market" is not fundamental analysis.

"I like their burgers/jeans/tacos/smartphones" is not fundamental analysis.

Okay smart guy, what is it then?

Fundamental analysis is an attempt to establish the *intrinsic* valuation of a business, using what you know about a company's business and the financial figures it publishes to show what the business should be worth.

Only then do you look at the share price. Obviously, you wouldn't want to buy the stock if it's higher than the intrinsic valuation. But, if it's the same, or mainly if it's lower, you might.

So, if you just buy a company because you like the product, that's not fundamental analysis. You don't know that the product makes money, how much it makes, or how the share price relates to that. (But if you like the product, research the company and its market, and *then* buy the stock, that's fundamental analysis. That's how famed fund manager Peter Lynch funded many of his best ideas.)

Suppose you buy a 'story stock' like Tesla, Internet stocks in 1999, or solar energy stocks. In that case, if you haven't done the numbers, again, that's not fundamental analysis. But if you come up with an idea of the numbers, then yes, it is.

Suppose you buy a stock by looking at what the share price has done in the past. In that case, that's not fundamental analysis (though it can still be a helpful tool for refining your timing, and we'll talk about that later).

And if you just buy what your friends tell you to, that not only isn't fundamental analysis, but it's a quick way to lose a lot of money.

So, to recap, if you're doing fundamental analysis, then you need to cover three factors:

- How good is the underlying business?
- How much should that business be worth?
- And is the value reflected in the share price?

Or to reduce the whole of fundamental analysis to a single question: "What is this business really worth?"

Why you need to understand Fundamental Analysis

You don't absolutely need to understand fundamental analysis. If you really find it too hard to do or don't have enough time, you can invest via ETFs for the long term. You will get (within a small margin of error) the same performance as the market that your ETF tracks. You can even buy ETFs that will pay you regular dividends.

But if you want to beat the market, as a long-term investor, you need to invest directly in stocks for at least part of your portfolio. And you'll need to understand fundamental analysis to do it well.

- You get a tip from a friend? You'll need to understand fundamental analysis to check it out and ensure the stock is worthwhile. (Often, it won't be.)
- You hear Warren Buffett is buying something? Even Warren Buffett gets it wrong sometimes (he's human, after all). You'll need fundamental analysis to ensure you agree with him about the stock.
- You like the burgers? First of all, you need to find out if the company is making money. Then, you need to work out what it's worth. That's fundamental analysis.

- There's a great story, like solar power? First, you need to check out the risks. How do solar energy suppliers set their prices? Could government action damage their business models? Are too many companies chasing the same business? Fundamental analysis will find out (and you should find the answers you're looking for in the company's annual report).
- If you're looking for fast growth, fundamental analysis will let you find stocks where earnings are likely to grow fast and the company has sufficient financial resources to cope with a fast-expanding business (some don't).
- If you're looking for the most profitable companies, you need to understand fundamental analysis to look for the right ratios.
- Fundamental analysis will let you look under the hood and check whether a company is as great as it says it is.
- Fundamental analysis will also let you check out whether management is telling the whole truth or hiding a few problem areas.
- And fundamental analysis can show you when a company is running out of cash.
- If you're looking for the cheapest companies, only fundamental analysis can deliver what you need.

Really, suppose you try to be a successful long-term investor without understanding fundamental analysis. In that case, you will rely a lot on your luck. But if you understand fundamental analysis, you will increase your percentage of good calls - and you should manage to reduce the unpleasant surprises very significantly.

The Origins of Fundamental Analysis

Even in the seventeenth century, when the Amsterdam and London Stock Exchanges led the world, merchants had worked out some way of analyzing the businesses they invested in. They didn't always get it right, as you'll know if you've heard about the South Sea Bubble (1720).

But the discipline of fundamental analysis as we know it today started in 1934 when Benjamin Graham published his first book, *Security Analysis*. Indeed, he's sometimes known as the father of fundamental analysis.

Graham was the first to formulate a complete methodological structure for the valuation of companies and stocks. At the same time, he preached *value investing*, which aims to look for stocks trading at 20% or more below what the analyst considers their intrinsic or fair value. He believed that this gave a good margin of error, which helps when dealing with the multiple uncertainties of forecasting company growth, economic growth, and stock markets.

However, you don't have to be a value investor to use fundamental analysis. Even if you prefer to invest in growth companies, fundamental analysis can help you avoid the companies that are at the highest risk, whether that's because their underlying business isn't very profitable, their debts are too high, or because they have management that is always too optimistic and never quite manages to do what they say they'll do.

The Pros and Cons of Fundamental Analysis

Like any technique, fundamental analysis has its advantages and disadvantages, and let's quickly sum them up.

Advantages:

- Value - Fundamental analysis allows you to find stocks priced at less than their actual value. It's letting you into the stock market's bargain basement.
- Risk avoidance - Fundamental analysis allows you to spot major risks such as an unsustainable level of debt, companies that are 'buying' sales (for instance, by giving customers extended credit terms), or enormous valuations.
- Lie detection - Doing fundamental analysis properly will ensure that you know exactly what you are buying. If you think you're buying a growth company, but you're actually buying a cash-burning business, it will tell you. If all the good stuff is in related companies, or the directors are doing dodgy deals, it will give you the best chance of finding out.
- Helps reduce churn - Churn, turning over your portfolio too rapidly has all sorts of costs, even if you use a zero-commission broker. It may create tax liabilities you don't want. By knowing all about the stocks you buy and weeding out the ones that don't qualify, you won't need to trade so often or watch your portfolio every day.
- Factual - Many of us let our emotions take a big part in investment decisions, even if we don't realize it. Fundamental analysis helps by focusing on factual data. For 'story stocks,' you can get beneath the glamorous story and test whether the engine is working.

Disadvantages:

- Time-consuming - Fundamental analysis takes time. It takes time to learn how to do it, and it takes time to do it. To analyze a single company properly could take a couple of evenings or a good part of your weekend.
- It can be dull. I hate to admit this, but even finance nerds find page 101 of the footnotes to the annual report tough going. There is no glamour in fundamental analysis. (Masters of the Universe probably don't bother with it.)
- It tells you **what** to buy, **not when** - I always love a clip of Peter Lynch talking about 'buying the dip'. He was a big buyer of Kaiser Corp at $26. then at $16. then at $14. Then at $10. Then at $3… the payoff? He did make money in the end because the stock split off all the different businesses and the payout added up to about $50 a share! Fundamental analysis will tell you *what* to buy, but it's not at all useful in telling you the right time to buy (That's where technical analysis comes in).
- It tends to look back rather than forwards. Looking at past years' financial reports will not necessarily help you if there's a significant disruption in the industry now. Even quarterly results come out several weeks after the end of the quarter.
- GIGO - As the nerds say, 'garbage in, garbage out'. If there's a fraud going on and the figures have been faked, analyzing them won't always be able to detect that - though sometimes you will get an inkling that things don't quite add up.

A little bit of philosophy

I should be honest here and tell you that many academics have questioned whether fundamental analysis works in achieving better performance than an asset allocation approach or a monkey picking stocks' names out of a hat. According to the *Efficient Market Theory*, stock markets are incredibly efficient at absorbing and interpreting new information, so at any given time, the share price reflects everything known about the company. If that's true, you can't know more than anyone else.

It's a nice theory. However, we live in the real world, and things aren't quite so simple.

First of all, the stock market is not driven by purely rational actors. It's often driven by emotions, of which the two most prominent are *fear and greed*. Those emotions can change overnight - as they did in the tech stock crash. One moment the market was saying, "The internet is growing really fast; these stocks will rocket," and the very next day, investors were saying, "None of these companies will ever make any money; we'd better look for the exit".

Secondly, while the Efficient Market Theory may work quite well for many of the biggest stocks, if you are interested in buying smaller, high-growth companies, you may find that the press or analysts do not cover them well. So, the assumption that the market knows all the facts probably doesn't work out in practice for these stocks.

If you're the only person to read all the way through the annual report, it is just possible you've come across something the market missed, or only a few people have noticed.

And thirdly, Ben Graham made money for his clients. Warren Buffett, who takes a fundamental analysis approach, has made himself a billionaire, as has his long-time business partner Charlie Munger. Peter Lynch, who ran Fidelity's Magellan Fund for many years, used fundamental analysis to become a consistent top performer among fund managers.

That suggests fundamental analysis can work rather well. I'm also pleased with the results it's delivered for my investments too.

Some examples of the Fundamental Analysis Toolbox

Let me give a few examples of the tools you might use in fundamental analysis. We'll talk about them in more detail in later chapters.

- Liquidity and debt ratios give you a way to pry open the company's bank accounts and find out whether it has too much debt, whether it can pay its interest expense, and whether it has the financial resources to cope with a cash crunch.
- Valuation ratios let you assess what you're paying for each dollar of earnings, or what dividend yield you'll get on your money invested. They also let you compare the stock you're interested in with others in the same line of business to find out if it's a good bargain or not.
- Closely reading the footnotes to the accounts shows you where the bodies are buried. All kinds of interesting wickedness goes on page 98 or so, and it's up to you to find it!
- Profitability ratios show you whether the company is as profitable as it should be, and whether it's becoming more or less profitable over time.
- Competitor analysis techniques help you decide whether the business you're buying has an advantage over its competitors - Warren Buffett calls this a 'moat' - and whether (and how) it's likely to grow.
- Return ratios help you see whether the company is making a return on its money invested that's above or below average - in other words, how successful it is at investing in its own business.

Chapter 1 Quiz

Just to check your understanding, every chapter in this book will have a short multiple-choice quiz at the end. Don't worry; no one's keeping the score, and you'll probably find that you do pretty well in most chapters. If you don't, all that's telling you is to re-read the chapter, maybe after a couple of days, and see if it makes better sense. The quiz answers are on page 269.

1. Fundamental analysis is
   a) A way of trading shares
   b) A form of psychotherapy
   c) Predicting how share prices will move
   d) Valuing the underlying business in which you buy shares

2. Who is the 'father of fundamental analysis'?
   a) Benjamin Franklin
   b) Cracker Graham
   c) Benjamin Graham
   d) Franklin Templeton

3. Which of these is *not* an advantage of using fundamental analysis?
   a) You can buy shares that are priced at less than fair value
   b) You might spot a problem with the business before the market does
   c) It's quick to do and requires no effort
   d) You can check whether management is telling the whole truth

4. Which of these is part of the fundamental analysis toolbox?
   a) Profitability ratio
   b) BMI
   c) Oscillator
   d) Graphological analysis of the CEO's signature

5. Which of these things won't fundamental analysis tell you?
   a) The company is running out of cash
   b) The shares are too highly priced
   c) The shares are going to go down tomorrow morning
   d) The company is growing fast

2

Chapter 2: Finding Fundamental Data

Things have really changed in the last 20 years or so. I'm certainly not ready to retire yet, but when I started trading, some of the older analysts were still working out their ratios with calculators and writing the results down in a notebook. One big change is this one:

- The old days: asking nicely for a report to be posted. One company wanted $3.50 for the report and postage - to be sent by check in the mail, as you would expect.
- Nowadays: the internet. Data on finance websites, the company's investor relations site, and the SEC site. And when you're done, don't ring your broker, just click the button on your broker's trading app to buy the shares.

So, finding the basic financial data is easy. That's the same for foreign stocks; for instance, stocks quoted on the London Stock Exchange have to file with the Regulatory News Service (RNS), and you can check their filings at www.londonstockexchange.com.

The same goes for French stocks, but the filings will be in French. If you don't speak French, the largest French stocks often have an ADR (basically, it's a way for U.S shareholders to buy the stock) listed on the New York Stock Exchange (NYSE), where you can find the filings. That's true, for instance, of French pharma stocks Sanofi and Valneva. The same is true for other foreign stocks, such as Japan's Toyota and Honda, China's biggest e-commerce stock Alibaba, India's IT stock Wipro, and many more.

If you have the filings, you have all the basic information to analyze a company. However, additional information may give you a richer and deeper appreciation of the business. Many companies produce a presentation for analysts that gives strategic long term predictions, information on the industry, and breakdowns of the business or its KPIs (key performance indicators) in addition to what's shown in the annual report.

Often, you can find industry-specific data here. The table on the next page has a few of these so you can see how specific some of them are. If you use these ratios, you're really getting to the heart of what makes that kind of business profitable.

Industry	KPIs
Airlines	ASK (available seat kilometers) = seats x distance flown RPK (revenue passenger kilometers) = ASK that were paid for
Retail	Sales per square foot Same-store sales
Media and telecoms	Customer acquisition cost Revenue per subscriber
Insurance	Persistency ratio (customer renewals) Solvency ratio (capital compared to claims) Incurred claims ratio (ratio of claims paid out in the year to the premium collected) Commission expense ratio
Hospitality	Occupancy ratio ADR = Average Daily Rate RevPAR = Revenue per available room
Services businesses	Revenue per employee Cost per employee

You'll also find a much more user-friendly graphical representation of business trends than you typically get in the annual report. So, it's worth seeing if these presentations are on the company's website, under 'Investor Relations'.

Why companies have to publish data

Private companies can get away with publishing very limited data. However, if a company wants to list its shares on the Stock Exchange, in return, it has to accept several commitments. One is publishing annual and quarterly reports up to a high standard. In some markets, such as the UK, bi-annual reporting (occurring twice a year) is more normal, but the same rules apply.

There are also rules about when companies need to issue other reports. For instance, if the company has information that will have a material effect on its results and share price, such as the cancellation of a major contract, or a downgrade in expectations for the year based on current performance, it needs to release a statement. Acquisitions also require a statement to be issued if they are above a certain size; Starbucks acquires a single coffee bar would not need to issue a statement, but if it wanted to acquire Dunkin' Donuts, it certainly would need to.

Imagine a stock market in which companies didn't need to publish this kind of data. Individual shareholders might not know that the CEO had just quadrupled his pay check, that the company was buying a competitor twice its size, and that it was so heavily in debt it would be lucky to survive the next 12 months. An analyst who knew the company and met its executives personally would know all these things.

Who do you think would have sold the shares before the company hit the skids? And who would be left with the worthless paper?

That's why these rules exist. They level the playing field and make sure everyone in the market knows what's going on, and have equally good information on which to base their investment decisions. In the U.S, they're policed by the SEC (Securities and Exchange Commission): financial regulators or the stock exchange in other countries.

You may have heard of the 'Pink Sheets' - an over-the-counter market that doesn't comply with these strict regulations. That's why a lot of smart people will tell you not to bother with the Pink Sheets; you have no way of checking that a company is achieving its objectives.

The Pink Sheets now tiers its stocks; 'International Premier QX' are pretty good (foreign shares which meet NYSE standards), but the bottom tier is named 'Caveat Emptor' (In Latin in means: 'Buyer, beware!') and has skull and crossbones as its symbol. That tells you all you need to know!

The financial data that have to be published are quite specific. There are also rules about other features that need to be included in the reports, particularly in the annual report, such as the management discussion and analysis of operations (MD&A), disclosures of executive compensation, and names of major shareholders, together with management shareholdings.

Why you should always read back to front

The front, or the top, of any earnings announcement or annual report is where management brag their stuff. It's where they feature the figures they are most pleased with (or least ashamed of), where they polish their image; it's publicity.

The footnotes are where they hide the things they don't want you to see. The footnotes are also where all the detailed information like sector breakdowns, debt maturities, and cash flow details are hidden. They put the spin first and the facts second.

That's why it's the footnotes you should read first. Always read back to front! (Okay, probably you should just have a quick look at the front page first, but then start looking at the footnotes.)

By the time you get to the front page, you'll be able to judge whether the summary gives you a fair picture of the company, or whether it's hopelessly over-optimistic.

What data companies have to publish

First of all, companies are required to publish their financial accounts, with a full income report (profit and loss account), balance sheet, and statement of cash flow. They're required to do that in the annual report, and they have to give some of this information in the quarterly reports (or in some markets, bi-annual reports). In the annual report, the results must have been audited by an accountancy firm, and come with extensive footnotes, some of which are mandatory, such as showing a breakdown of debts, while others are optional, such as sector breakdowns.

Companies are also required to publish the agenda for the annual stockholder meeting (or any other big meetings needed, for instance, to decide on a major share issue or an acquisition). In the U.S, this is called the proxy statement, and the SEC calls it by the catchy name of Form DEF 14A. Shareholders are entitled to vote on the proposals.

Let's look at the different forms that need to be submitted to the SEC. You'll notice that the SEC is not imaginative when it comes to names.

- 8K – Companies required to announce any unscheduled events (such as acquisitions or the need to write off an investment) or corporate changes within four days of the event. Companies also often issue an 8k as a preliminary report or trading statement just after the end of a quarter, talking about how things have gone but without giving a full financial breakdown.

- 10Q - This form shows the firm's business and financial performance each quarter, and it's not audited. (In the last quarter, the 10K takes its place).
- 10K - the comprehensive annual report, including an overview of the business, risk factors, financial data, MD&A, and audit report.
- Schedule 13D - This report must be produced whenever an owner acquires more than 5% of the shares in the company.
- Forms 3, 4 and 5 show if insiders are buying or selling stock in the company.
- Form 144 shows proposed sales of restricted stock.
- DEF 14A - Proxy statement, which we already talked about.

Most companies also produce an annual report for shareholders that is prettier than the 10K and has pictures and some supplementary information. But it will still have the 10K included in the back (often on cheaper, non-glossy paper). The corporate glossy report is good for understanding how the company wants to present itself, but most of the real information is in the boring-looking 10K.

All these forms can be accessed through the SEC's Electronic Data Gathering, Analysis, and Retrieval system. For once, the SEC has a catchy name for something - EDGAR! You'll find this fantastic source of information at:

www.sec.gov/edgar/searchedgar/companysearch.html

If you're a bit of a geek, you may want to download statements in XBRL, an XML standard that tags financial reporting data so that you can easily process them in a spreadsheet or database.

The rules are similar for companies quoted on the Euronext exchanges in London and Tokyo, though they differ in detail. For instance, London stocks only have to issue two statements a year (not quarterly), accounting details are different, some of the names of accounts differ (e.g. statement of comprehensive income vs profit and loss account), and the exact format of releases differs. But they all have to release detailed accounting data and a discussion of operations at regular intervals.

Why proxy statements and Forms 3,4, & 5 and 144 are useful

Proxy statements can be dry as dust. They are a document the SEC requires companies to provide shareholders that includes information needed to make decisions at shareholder meetings. Very often, they are business-as-usual. They simply ask stockholders to reappoint some of the directors, reappoint the auditors, and approve the accounts. That's it. The same motions and even the same words as last year. This kind of proxy statement you can usually ignore.

But sometimes, a proxy statement shows that storms are brewing. For instance, an activist shareholder such as Carl Icahn or Nelson Peltz might want to appoint a director of their own choice to the board. They may even want to overthrow the entire management or stop the company from making what they think will be a disastrous or risky acquisition. So, proxy statements are well worth reading because they show the fault lines in the company.

Proxy statements also have to detail related party transactions. An example might be where a company lends money to one of its customers, and that customer uses the money to buy or lease the company's product. I've seen that happen several times, and every time I've spotted it in a company I covered, that company ended up losing money for shareholders. (If you imagine going to a bar where the landlord lent everyone money to pay for their drinks... it wouldn't keep going long, so you'd want to enjoy it while you could!) Or the company might employ a consultancy in which the CEO holds a significant stake. Would you think the company is getting good value for money? Or would you guess the CEO is making more out of it than the company is getting in benefit?

In the proxy statement, you'll also get a rundown of who the executives are and what they get paid.

As for insider buying and selling, it's often an indication of the amount (or lack of) confidence management have in the company. Even though they're not allowed to trade based on inside information - such as selling the shares just before bad results come out - insiders generally have a good feeling for the general direction in which the company's going.

Watch out, particularly for Form 144. Companies often issue restricted stock to executives and employees during their IPOs. These stocks can't be sold during a lock-in period (the period during which investors are not allowed to redeem or sell their investments), say six months or a year. But at the end of that time, you may see large amounts of stock coming on to the market as insiders sell out.

That's not always a sign that they are negative about the company's future. If let's say, you're just a marketing assistant at HotStartup.com, but you end up with shares worth $10m, then it's easy to understand why you might want to sell some of that and pay off your home loan. But if a large number of shares come on the market, it will still probably depress the share price. (I mean, there may be a good reason for a large number of shares coming on the market. It's not necessarily a sign that management is selling out because the company is hitting the skids. But that's still going to hurt the market because firstly, there's more supply, and secondly, traders will see the sale of shares and jump to negative conclusions, and sell their shares too which would depress the share price.)

The earnings season

Most companies will have a December year-end. That means their results will all come out at roughly the same time, with annual results coming out in late February or early March. Similarly, most quarterly reports will cluster around dates around three weeks to a month after the end of the quarter. (The SEC's official deadline is 40 days.)

In the retail sector, a December year-end would bring way too much pressure because of the clustering of sales around Black Friday, Thanksgiving, and Christmas. Many retail companies draw up their accounts at the end of January instead.

This is the busiest time of year for analysts and should also be the busiest time of year for investors. Some days, several companies you look at will report at once. However, you don't need to feel that you have to read the whole 10K within a few minutes of its publication. Usually, traders read the headline, journalists read the front page, and only analysts read the whole report (one thing you learn quickly as an analyst is that traders can't read more than three lines of text before their attention span ends). Often, the direction a stock took after the results can reverse on the next day of trading; that's because the analysts have found something interesting buried on page 10, or they've done a bit more work and don't like what they've found out.

One of the most important things to understand when you're looking at how share prices behave in the earnings season is that the stock market is driven by expectations. Analysts will already have made their forecasts for the quarter. Earnings tend to be assessed by whether they meet, exceed, or fall short of that forecast. We say, for instance, that a company "missed its earnings" or delivered "a positive earnings surprise".

So always make a practice, *before* the earnings are due out, to use a service like Yahoo Finance or Zacks and look up what the analyst expectation is for the quarter. Then you'll be able to make the same immediate assessment of the figures as anyone in the stock market.

By the way, those sites will also give you a financial calendar, as well as MarketWatch - and each individual company's investor relations website. That lets you be sure nothing gets under your radar!

Where else to get useful data

Wall Street and City analysts usually benefit from the chance of a phone call or Zoom meeting with management on the day of the results. That used to be a huge advantage for the professional analyst over the retail investor, but now it's become common for companies to open up the call to retail investors, or to record the meeting and have a recording plus a transcript available on the company's website. You can also find analyst calls on fool.com and other finance websites.

These are definitely worth listening to. You're not going to get any insider information, as executives know they're not allowed to give out non-public information that could affect the share price. But there are other advantages to listening to the analysts' call. First of all, the participants will often go into more detail about operational aspects of the business than you might have found in the report.

There's also usually a PowerPoint presentation which will often contain plenty more detail. As I mentioned, they often have neat charts too. Make sure if you're going to listen to a transcript that you print out the presentation, or download it to your laptop first.

Make a particular note of any other companies or new technologies or products that the company talks about. You can look them up later and find out more.

But of course, a company will usually only talk about itself and its own products. If you want a different view, find its competitors and look up what they have to say. Reading one company's report is like going to the top of a mountain; you get a wonderful view, but you can't see everything in the landscape because you can't see into dips or past the nearest hills. Climb another mountain a few miles away and while it's the same landscape, you'll be able to see a few things you couldn't see from the other peak. You've also got a chance to check whether that hill over there looks as high as it did from the other peak - to triangulate your observations and confirm them.

That's why you want to pull up data on companies that compete with the one you're analyzing and listen to their calls too.

Analysts' reports

If you get a chance, you should definitely look at analysts' reports on the company. There are two good reasons to do so:

- In the case of regular 'information' reports, you get the earnings forecasts. You need to see the latest forecasts to know what the market expects for the next results season. However, you can also get the consensus forecasts from finance websites.
- Larger reports, initiating coverage or looking at major events, will include a detailed breakdown of the business and its prospects. These reports are really worth looking at as you can see how a professional analyst looks at the business, what kind of ratios they're using and what comparisons they think are most useful. Industry reports are particularly worth reading, as they cover numerous companies and often have insights into the direction of the industry as a whole.

Many analysts publish a 'year in focus' report. Saxo Bank also makes a series of 'Outrageous Predictions' at the start of a new year (just Google 'Saxo bank outrageous predictions'). I love these because they really make you think. In fact, some of them are not so outrageous after all!

Additionally, sometimes analysts will explore the different bases of valuation that might be applied. This can occasionally be the best part of the report. For instance, moving from valuing a railroad company as a transportation stock to looking at it as a potential source of real estate values might make a huge difference to the valuation.

These reports are usually directed to institutional investors such as pension funds and mutual fund managers. However, some services allow you to access them for a fee, while some large brokers offer access as part of client perks - Merrill Edge, for instance, gives you access to Merrill's analyst reports as well as Morningstar.

You might also want to look at what the credit analysts are saying. The major credit rating agencies - Fitch, S&P and Moody's - are paid to rate every bond issued by a company. Their clients are banks and bond investors, and their objective differs from equity analysts. In brief, you could say that equity analysts want to make their clients money, while credit analysts want to stop their clients from losing it. Equity analysts are quite bullish by nature and default to 'hold' as their worst recommendation, while credit analysts are naturally pessimistic and will tend to err on the downside.

Credit reports are a great reality check. If you're looking at a company with fast growth in revenues, and a good story to tell, but the credit report tells you all the financial trends are getting worse and the bonds are rated as junk, you may just have saved yourself a lot of money.

As with annual reports, I prefer to read analyst reports back to front. Ignore the recommendation; look at the numbers first, and the assumptions the analyst used in forecasting them. Then read the body of the text. Finally, look at the front page. (The way recommendations are reported in news media is completely useless to a fundamental analyst. It doesn't matter that Goldman Sachs has changed a hold to a buy recommendation; what matters is *why*, and they rarely tell you that!)

The only time a recommendation has ever been interesting was when a UK media analyst called Derek Terrington was looking at Mirror Group Newspapers - a group run by Bob Maxwell, a larger-than-life character who ended up floating in the sea, after which it was discovered he was effectively bankrupt. Terrington had his suspicions and decided that although he wasn't allowed to make a 'sell' recommendation, he would give good advice. His recommendation was original: "Cannot Recommend A Purchase."

You might like to go back and look at the capital letters of those 4 last words...

The bond markets

Many large companies have a number of bonds in issue. The bond markets work rather differently from the equity markets, but you can find out how bonds are trading through FINRA Trace, which reports bond prices.

You can then work out the current yield on the bond. For example, a 5% bond issued at par, at $100, and that's now trading at $50, would currently yield 10%. (So basically the 5% bond at $100 par = $5 payment. And then the $5 payment on the new $50 trading price = 10% current yield.)

Of course, if the bond price has doubled to $200, the yield has halved to 2.5%. ($5 payment / $200 bond x 100 = 2.5% new yield).

The $5 payment is set by the company on the issue price. So, it will remain the same, whatever happens to the market price. It's like having a fixed rate mortgage.

Bond traders will tell you that calculation is simplistic, but it's good enough for us.

Now you just have to compare the yield with the rest of the market. The difference is called the *spread*. If, let's say, Bankrupt Corp bonds are trading at 8% while 10-year Treasuries are trading at 1%, that tells you something important about the bond market's view of Bankrupt Corp. It can be particularly useful to see if the spread is getting wider or narrower. A pronounced widening trend would tell you that the market is getting increasingly worried about the company's ability to pay, so it wants to be paid a higher and higher coupon for the risk.

On the other hand, a company that starts to get its balance sheet in shape and starts to make a profit again will usually see the spread narrowing, as investors realize they aren't running such a high risk and can accept a lower return.

Other information

Finally, let's not forget other sources of information which won't necessarily tell you directly about the company, but will help you understand the industry sector and also give you some useful comparisons to see just how well the company that you're analyzing is performing. Briefly, you might look at:

- Industry journals, such as AdAge (advertising), Aviation Week, Women's Wear Daily, Packaging World, or sites like HotelBusiness.com. They often have articles that look at trends in the sector on a broad scale, which can be very helpful when you're learning about an industry. They also cover what the biggest private operators in the sector are doing - information that you won't find on the stock exchange.
- Actually, 'kicking the tires'. That's easy to do with consumer businesses, for instance, go and stay in hotels, eat in restaurants, buy the clothes (or ask friends and colleagues what they think of them). But you can also visit show homes for residential developments, for instance. One analyst employed someone who lived opposite a factory to count the number of trucks coming in and going out, to see how much business the firm was doing!
- Many major accounting and consulting firms have sector reviews on their websites. These can sometimes be rather theoretical, but other times they're quite interesting in talking about factors such as factory automation, demographic change, regulation and government action, and venture capital funding coming into the sector. Usually, you'll know by reading the abstract whether it's worth reading the whole report.
- Trade shows and exhibitions can be a good place to head if you want to see what's happening in the industry. However, remember not to be distracted - you're there to find out what's happening and how products are emerging, not to collect corporate ballpoint pens. Be honest and introduce yourself as an individual investor, and find the people who can tell you how things work, not the people who have been hired in to front the stands. If you find good contacts, keep them forever.

- Some people like using LinkedIn to find contacts in the sectors they cover. I must admit that it doesn't work well for me, but, as they say, "Your Mileage May Vary".

Make sure you understand the business model

Before you start crunching numbers, make sure you know the business model. For instance, do Chipotle and McDonald's have the same business model?

No, they don't! Chipotle owns and manages the vast majority of its own restaurants. McDonald's, on the other hand, operates through a franchise model. Though from the street they look like similar businesses, when you look at the business model and the cash flows, they work differently. Chipotle is a typical retailer, taking what you pay for your meal in revenue and then paying staff costs, rent and the cost of ingredients. McDonald's, on the other hand gets someone else to run each individual business, pay the rent, pay the staff, and take the money, and McDonald's takes a franchise fee when they start up, plus a share of their income every year.

So, what are McDonald's costs? They're all what you might call 'head office costs' - running finances, setting up the operating procedures, developing new recipes and offers, marketing, and training their franchisees.

Where do you think Aéroports de Paris (Paris Airports) makes its money? Think hard before you answer that question.

In the third quarter of 2021, it made more than half its income from retailing and real estate. Aviation fees made up less than half. And nearly a fifth of its revenue came from international airports. In fact, the biggest growth came from Amman, in Jordan, and Almaty, in Kazakhstan - Paris was virtually flat.

Don't ever trust a company name to tell you how it makes its money or where it makes its money; "what it says on the tin" can be highly misleading!

Chapter 2 Quiz

1. Which of these is not an SEC filing?
   a. 10K
   b. 10Q
   c. C3PO
   d. Form 144

2. Which way should you read the annual report?
   a. Back to front
   b. Upside down
   c. Only odd numbered page
   d. In one sitting

3. What is the big problem with Pink Sheet stocks?
   a. They are small
   b. They are only in risky industries
   c. They are pink
   d. They don't have to publish information

4. What is MD&A?
   a. Mergers Disposals & Acquisitions
   b. A dangerous drug
   c. Management's Discussion & Analysis of operations
   d. Marketing, Differentiation & Advertising

5. What is the 10K?
   a. A running race
   b. The annual report SEC filing
   c. An addendum to the quarterly report
   d. A footnote to the accounts

Fundamental Analysis for Beginners

48

3

Chapter 3: Beat the Street

You may believe that the odds are stacked against you. Surely, big banks and brokers with their highly paid teams of analysts, huge trading teams, expertise and information... Surely, they are going to beat you hands down every time?

Well, that's not exactly true! And there are quite a number of reasons why.

Professional constraints vs single-minded motivation

For a start, consider motivation. What's yours? To make money.

But that's not what motivates analysts or fund managers. Fund managers are under pressure to ensure they don't underperform the market. They also have regulatory pressures - for instance, they may not be allowed to invest in smaller stocks. And because one of fund management companies' big concerns is AUM (assets under management), they'll launch funds in whatever is today's flavor in order to get more customers - whether that's tech, 'green' investing, high income, whatever.

In fact, cynics often say you can tell when a bubble is about to crash by the number of new funds being launched!

Other funds are 'benchmarked'. That means the fund manager has to reflect the relevant index, for instance, the S&P 500. That could mean they are forced to invest in the biggest stocks in the market; they can decide to have, for example, less Tesla and more Alphabet, less Coca-Cola and more PepsiCo, but they can't make any really big bets. An index fund is a fund which is created to match the performance of a given stock market index, such as the S&P 500 or the FTSE 100. (On the other hand, a benchmarked fund measures its performance against the index, but the fund manager can overweight or underweight stocks or sectors to try to achieve better performance. Of course, sometimes fund managers don't do better; they do worse.)

Analysts are driven by the need to create a 'story'; sometimes one analyst will break cover with a big sell story, and they may be right (it's always worth looking at these standout recommendations), but they're motivated mainly because if they get it right, they will have made their name. But analysts are also driven by the agenda of the bank they work for; they may be told to 'go gently' with a stock because it's a corporate finance customer, for instance.

Analysts also have to worry about their competition. Can they get to the number one spot in the Institutional Investor research rankings? Whereas you don't care at all about that kind of thing - you just want to make money in the long term.

You also don't have to worry about quarterly performance. You don't have a boss who will fire you if a stock sits out for a while - you can afford to take a long term view. You don't have to track the market. You make your own decisions, for your own benefit.

And that's why you can beat the market.

Fund managers' constraints: why size is important

Many mutual funds are massive in size. In the UK, for instance, Fundsmith Equity Fund has a total market capitalization of £24.8bn - there are only 11 companies in the FTSE 100 index that it wouldn't have enough money to buy! But that's chicken feed compared to the USA's biggest mutual fund, Vanguard Total Stock Market Index Fund Admiral Shares, which has assets under management of $921bn, way ahead of its next rival, the Fidelity 500 Index Fund, which manages a tiny sum of $274bn.

Of course, these funds are by far the biggest, and the fund universe goes all the way down to boutique funds with just a few million dollars invested, often niche funds investing in a single country (like Vietnam) or a single subsector (like nanotechnology or REITs - Real Estate Investment Trust). But there are a lot of large funds, and their sheer size means they have to choose a large minimum size of investment - too big for many smaller companies.

Add to this the fact that most funds have strict limits on the percentage of a company that they can purchase, and you end up with many smaller and even mid-sized companies which just aren't possible candidates for the biggest funds.

For instance, the Fidelity Magellan Fund, with $32bn under management at the end of 2021, had a mathematical average holding size of nearly $500m (with 69 total holdings).

Suppose we find a small cap company - that means all its shares, at the current share price, would be worth below $2bn. Even if the company is right at the top of the range, Magellan's average holding would represent 25% of the company's total stock (if it took its average holding of $500m - that's 25% of $2bn). So, it's unlikely that any fund of that size would be interested in researching a small cap stock.

Table below shows the capitalization of different sizes of stock

Stock size	Market capitalization
Big cap	$10bn plus
Mid cap	$2-10bn
Small cap	Below $2bn
Micro-cap	$50-300m
Nano-cap	Below $50m

There's also an issue for funds that don't have their own dedicated research team, if they buy stocks that are not covered by a good number of analysts. Without in-depth research coverage, the fund could be accused of having been unprofessional or even negligent in its investment strategy if the investment goes wrong. So, such funds tend to stick to the larger and well-researched stocks, which are covered by numerous analysts and on which a lot of research reports are available.

You, on the other hand, can choose whatever size of company you like. If you do your research properly, and you don't pick obvious choices that have got popular on social trading or Reddit, you can bet that very few people outside the small boutique funds are doing so. That means, to go back to the Efficient Market Theory, you're taking maximum advantage of the market inefficiencies in the small cap market. But it also means you need to do your research properly!

Oh, another small thing. Because an analyst of an investment bank is publishing their research, they have to get absolutely *everything* calculated and forecast, even if it's not material (technical definition: won't account for more than 5% of costs, revenue or profits). You don't. If you've satisfied yourself, for instance, that stock-based compensation isn't important with the company you're looking at, or that the 'other' item isn't worth forecasting and never has been, just leave them out! That is, if these items are really small and aren't going to impact the earnings figures, you can just not bother looking at them or putting them in the spreadsheet - analysts have to show everything, but an investor can do a back-of-envelope calculation.

Taking the emotion out of investment

You'd think the professionals are cold-blooded, wouldn't you? But actually - and I speak from experience - being too close to the market can mess around with your mind. For a start, every sell-side analyst (working for a broker, not a fund) is close to a trading desk, and when the trading desk is roaring away, it's easy to get caught up in the excitement. And, of course, that trading desk will watch the stock price every second. If the stock falls 2% in early trading, someone will phone the analyst to find out why. You don't get much peace in that job.

Any financial trading center is also quite self-contained, which helps groupthink take hold. Since it's a little world of its own, it's easy for a consensus to be created which doesn't actually reflect reality, and it can be difficult to go against it. It's difficult to ignore the current narratives and come up with an independent view.

Fundamental Analysis for Beginners

While analysts may be quite honest in setting their target values for stocks, it can be difficult to be the only person with a very different view from the market.

Besides, getting things wrong carries major penalties, whether you're an analyst or a fund manager. It can affect your career and even lead to your termination, which can involve public shame. 'Maverick' fund managers who have taken a minority view often don't survive the first six months of underperformance before their strategy starts to pay off - they're attacked in the press, and their employer lets them go. No wonder most analysts and fund managers want to follow the crowd, or at least not be so far out of step with the market that they run any significant risks.

You have an easy way to take emotion out of your investments. Simply don't look at the share prices. Don't look at finance TV shows. Don't log on to your broker every day. Just ignore all this noise and the emotions connected with them.

As a fundamental analyst, you can afford to do that because:

- you're looking for long term investment ideas, perhaps with a 5-10 year horizon or even longer;
- you've probably bought stocks at 10-20% less than they're worth;
- you care about the intrinsic value of the stock, not the market value.

Having your own target price

When you're in the market, you're always looking at the latest move up or down. It's easy to forget about the intrinsic value of the stock.

You, on the other hand, have worked out what the business is actually worth. If a stock that you thought was too expensive falls a little, it might end up at your buy price. Assuming that the fundamentals haven't changed, you are happy buying - because you named your own price.

What you've done is exactly the same as saying, "That new Ford pickup is too expensive at $30,000. I'm gonna wait a few months and see if the price comes down." If you've been waiting for a new model to be reduced in the dealerships, when at last it's discounted, you don't say, "Oh, but that proves it's not a good pickup at all," do you? No, you snap it up!

You'd be surprised how often people look at a share price falling and think it's time to sell. (Very occasionally, when a share price plummets for no good reason - and I mean plummets, like 20% or 30% in a couple of days - you should take notice; someone, somewhere, knows something.) In fact, 'buy on the dips' is great - as long as you have the patience to wait for the stock to start performing again, and enough left in the bank to buy even more if it keeps heading downwards for a while.

Well, Peter Lynch got away with it, but most fund managers would be facing some very awkward questions from their employers - and possibly also from investors in their funds!

Specialist knowledge

Maybe you think you need specialized knowledge to find the right stocks. For some stocks, you certainly will. For instance, if you have never even managed to find your way onto Facebook and think Twitter is for the birds, you probably should give social media stocks a miss. And it's difficult to value pharmaceutical stocks unless you have at least some basic knowledge about how both drugs and the health system work.

That's why you should ensure before buying a stock that you fully understand its products and business model.

However, you may actually have some specialist knowledge that you haven't given yourself credit for. For instance, if you work in retail, you probably have a very good idea of evaluating other retail businesses in terms of their stores' size, attraction, and siting, and how well their products play to their intended market. As I write this, Meta (the renamed Facebook) has lost $230bn off its market capitalization in a massive single-day plunge. But the first signs of problems were already there - not only was Facebook getting into regulatory trouble, but when I asked my friends' kids if they used Facebook, they looked at me as if I was crazy. They're all TikTokers now. Having teenage kids, apparently, makes you a good social media analyst!

And, of course, if you're a doctor, you probably have an edge on the rest of us if you invest in pharmaceutical stocks. You know what you're doing. At least, we hope so!

This is also somewhere your friends can help. Don't listen to stock tips from your friends - but do listen to what they're telling you about their jobs and about products they buy and use.

- "My firm's given up using that software because it's fallen behind in functionality over the past few years."
- "You're not serious? No one shops at Gap anymore!"

- "Seriously, I know everyone thinks that town is stuck in the mud, but new stores are opening all the time, and there's a huge amount of construction happening."
- "The store where we get building supplies just put up the price of plumbing copper pipe by nearly half!"
- "They don't have any second-hand cars left in inventory at the dealers, we're going to have to buy new."

These kinds of comments can give you valuable insights into the market. It was actually the prices of second-hand cars that made Peter Lynch think about one of his best investments in the auto industry, just when everyone had decided that the car makers were all going bankrupt. He realized there was more demand for potential buyers than the car makers could supply - and the market was about to turn.

By the way, you can also leverage this kind of specialized knowledge by joining an investment club. If you enjoy working with other people rather than on your own, it will be worth your while anyway - you'll be happier with a social background for your investment journey. www.betterinvesting.org is your hub for contacting local investment clubs and finding out more.

Chapter 3 Quiz

1. Analysts' recommendations can be affected by all except one of
    these factors.
    a. Other relationships between the bank they work for and
        the company they analyze,
    b. Not wanting to go too far from the consensus,
    c. Something they ate the night before,
    d. Wanting to make their name by a bold recommendation.

2. What's the definition of a mid cap stock?
    a. A stock with $2-10bn market capitalization,
    b. A stock with less than $500m capitalization,
    c. One of the ten biggest stocks on the exchange,
    d. A stock with a skull and crossbones symbol.

3. Which of these is not a retail investor advantage?
    a. Being unconstrained in investment choice,
    b. Having a long term investment horizon,
    c. Having more time to devote to the market,
    d. Not having to hit quarterly targets.

4. Your friends can help you by
    a. Giving you stock tips,
    b. Lending you money to invest,
    c. Giving you the benefit of their specialist knowledge,
    d. Giving you insider information.

5. Why should you be investing in stocks?
    a. To achieve above average performance,
    b. To make money,
    c. To impress people,
    d. To track the market.

A.Z Penn

4

Chapter 4: The three types of statements you need to know, and where to find them

In this chapter, I'm going to show you the three financial statements you need to know to analyze a company. I'll also talk about how much each one of them can tell you about the health of a company - and where to find them in the annual report and other filings.

The three statements are:

- the income statement - what profit the company is making,
- the balance sheet - what the company owns and owes, and
- the cash flow statement - what actually went through the bank account (and I'll explain why that's *not* the same as the profit the company made).

You'll find all the statements under Item 8 of the 10K filing, 'Financial statements and supplementary data'. To make life much easier than it use to be, SEC filings now come with internal hyperlinks to each section - the days of having to scroll through pages and pages of text are gone forever!

What I'm going to do here is to base our work on a single company's annual report, so that you get used to hopping around it and seeing how the different parts relate to the whole. It's Amazon's annual report for 2020, available on the company's investor relations website. Simply type in "Amazon investor relation" on your browser, then on the left side of the website, click "Annual reports, proxies and shareholder letters". You can find it by clicking "2021", and then "2020 Annual Report". You might want to download it, or even print it off. Here's the link for you anyway;

https://ir.aboutamazon.com/annual-reports-proxies-and-shareholder -letters/default.aspx

It's stated according to GAAP - Generally Accepted Accounting Principles. Rather than a set of rules, it's more a framework of standards for accounting, so it does allow quite a lot of caution to accountants and auditors.

I'm going to take you through each of the three main statements of accounts separately. But I'd like to warn you never to look at any one of the statements in isolation from the others. All three are interconnected.

By the way, in my free bonus #1 - Company Valuation Simplified Masterclass, I walk you through some of the financial statements discussed in this chapter and share my real-time analysis on a company called Vesta. It would be practical for you to watch this masterclass to gain a better idea on how to think like an analyst. Please visit www.az-penn.com to watch the class.

Income Statement

The income statement is referred to as the 'consolidated statement of operations'. 'Consolidated' because if the company owns smaller subsidiaries, those are all included in the accounts.

And below is what one looks like. It's on page 39 of Amazon's 10k for the Consolidated Statement of Operations in 2020.

AMAZON.COM, INC.
CONSOLIDATED STATEMENTS OF OPERATIONS
(in millions, except per share data)

	Year Ended December 31,		
	2018	2019	2020
Net product sales	$ 141,915	$ 160,408	$ 215,915
Net service sales	90,972	120,114	170,149
Total net sales	232,887	280,522	386,064
Operating expenses:			
Cost of sales	139,156	165,536	233,307
Fulfillment	34,027	40,232	58,517
Technology and content	28,837	35,931	42,740
Marketing	13,814	18,878	22,008
General and administrative	4,336	5,203	6,668
Other operating expense (income), net	296	201	(75)
Total operating expenses	220,466	265,981	363,165
Operating income	12,421	14,541	22,899
Interest income	440	832	555
Interest expense	(1,417)	(1,600)	(1,647)
Other income (expense), net	(183)	203	2,371
Total non-operating income (expense)	(1,160)	(565)	1,279
Income before income taxes	11,261	13,976	24,178
Provision for income taxes	(1,197)	(2,374)	(2,863)
Equity-method investment activity, net of tax	9	(14)	16
Net income	$ 10,073	$ 11,588	$ 21,331
Basic earnings per share	$ 20.68	$ 23.46	$ 42.64
Diluted earnings per share	$ 20.14	$ 23.01	$ 41.83
Weighted-average shares used in computation of earnings per share:			
Basic	487	494	500
Diluted	500	504	510

The first thing you may notice is that it gives you three years of data - for 2018, 2019 and 2020. That's really useful as it lets you look at trends rather than just having two data points. I always like to see if I can get a five-year run of figures - if I got the 2018 report, I'd have 2017 and 2016 figures too, which would really give me confidence in whatever trends I have noted.

- If I only had two years of data, for instance, if sales went up between 2019 and 2020, that might just be because 2019 had been a particularly bad year. In fact, 2020 sales might still be below 2018 levels for all I'd know.
- If I had three years of data, I'd see whether there was a steady trend. So, if in 2019 sales were up 20% and in 2020, they were up 15%, yes, there's an upwards trend. But I might not have a good feeling for whether it was slowing down or whether that's just a normal variance.
- Suppose I get the additional two years of data of 2016 and 2017, and I see that previously, sales have risen by 15% and 18%, then I could see that 2020 is perfectly normal. On the other hand, if I saw that sales had risen by 70% in 2017, then 35% in 2018, then 20%, then 15%, I know the trend is slowing down.

As Oscar Wilde might have said, "To have one bad quarter might be regarded as a misfortune; to have two looks like carelessness."

You might also want to calculate CAGR - the Compound Annual Growth Rate. This averages out growth over, say, a three or five year period, ironing out all the intermediate ups and downs.

The formula is the difference between the final figure and the figure at the beginning, to the power of 1/number of years, minus 1. See below:

$$\text{CAGR} = \left(\frac{V_{\text{final}}}{V_{\text{begin}}} \right)^{1/t} - 1$$

But never mind all that, there are loads of CAGR calculators on the internet, and a function in most spreadsheet packages. (CAGR is particularly interesting if you want to get a long term growth rate you can use in forecasting.)

In the screenshot below, I have a CAGR calculator using cagrcalculator.net to work out the sales CAGR from the Amazon 2020 income statement.

CAGR (Compound Annual Growth Rate)	15.01 %
Starting value: (Initial Investment Value)	141915
Ending value: (Ending Investment Value)	215915
No. of periods: (Months/Years)	3
Calculate	
CAGR (Compound Annual Growth Rate)	15.01 %

Over the course of 3 years/months your investment grew from **141915.0** to **215915.0**. Its compound annual growth rate (CAGR) is **15.01** %.

I used the sales figures for 2018 and 2020, and the time period was three years (2018, 2019 and 2020). It gives us a 15.01% CAGR. It's as simple as that to calculate!

Okay, so now I'm going to look at Amazon's Consolidation of Operations, from the top to show you how the income statement works. Basically, it's all about subtraction. We start at the top with sales (or revenues); it's nice to see that they are growing steadily. (Let's not worry about the split between product and service sales for the moment - we'll look at that in the next chapter. For now, focus on the *total net sales*). So this is all the company's sale, everything coming into the company, and as we go down the statement, we'll be subtracting various costs till at the bottom we get the profit, or *net income* for the year. (In some instances, there may be a few additions instead of subtractions, for example, if the company has money in the bank, it might have *interest income*, which would need to be added rather than subtracted.)

Sales/revenues is "the top line".

Next comes the *operating expenses*. These are the regular expenses the business incurs, such as cost of sales, payroll, head office, marketing, etc. Here they are split in a rather different way.

- *Cost of sales* relates to the direct costs of business. For instance, with a retailer like Walmart, cost of sales is what Walmart pays for its supplies - in that case, I always like to work out *gross profit*, which is revenue deduct cost of sales. That shows whether Walmart is managing to keep its mark-up stable over time (the money it makes on each item before it starts paying for the store's and the business's cost).
- *Fulfillment covers* costs of Amazon's logistics network - sending stuff out to customers.
- *Technology and content* includes all the tech costs. If you do a bit of research on Amazon's business model, you'll find that the tech doesn't just cover the cost of Amazon's e-commerce site, but also Amazon Cloud services (AWS) which it provides to third parties.
- *Marketing* includes all the costs of promoting the company's products and services. It's worth keeping an eye on - some businesses cut marketing costs to push up short-term profits, but then they see their revenues have no growth. That's happened to Kraft Heinz and brewer Anheuser-Busch, for instance.
- *General and administrative* are all the other costs of the business. Watch this line - sometimes you can see how a company is getting bloated and wasteful. If this line expands more than all the others, either a growing company has taken a step up (a new headquarters, new accounting system, new and more experienced board), or the executives are not keeping an eye on costs.
- *Other operating expenses* is the amount which generally does not depend on sales or production quantities. Go to page 29 on their annual report and you'll find out what this figure represents.

Take away all of these *operating expenses* from the *net sales*, and you have *operating income* - the basic profitability of the business, before we start thinking about debt service or taxation. This is a good level at which to compare businesses. (However, as you'll see in the next chapter, accounting treatments can make a difference at this level and we might want to make a few adjustments.)

Next comes finance - *interest income* and *interest expense*. Most companies have both cash in the bank, on which they collect interest, and debt, on which they pay out interest. That's the case here; in fact, Amazon pays more interest than it collects. Take a look at the interest paid of $1,647m and operating income of $22,899m, and you can see that Amazon isn't in trouble here - it makes enough profit to service its debt several times over (13.9 times over, that's $22,899m/$1,647m).

Also included at this level is *other income*. This usually isn't very significant, but look at Amazon's 2020 result - it's a nice little slug of extra income. I might want to take a look at the footnotes, or the MD&A, to find out what that represents. But it's probably a currency adjustment or a revaluation of warrants, something like that.

Once the financial and other costs are removed from operating income (or in 2020, financial and other income is added to it as *total non-operating income*), you have *Income before income tax*. Take a look at that line and you can see it's growing strongly - it made a really big jump in 2020. I wonder why? (Let's find out in the next chapter when we look at ratios.)

After that comes a *provision for income taxes*. This isn't the same as tax paid. It means Amazon's accountants have sat down and worked out what they need to pay the IRS when they file. Then they have made an allowance for that. So, this isn't cash that has actually gone out of the business, it's what's *expected* to be paid.

If you think that's a bit odd, let me introduce you to the *accrual system* of accounting (which I will discuss in more detail in the next section).

The income statement is about what the company made in the period, but it's not about cash coming in and out - and that's why, later in this chapter, I'm going to take you through the *cash flow statement*.

There's also a very small item called *equity-method investment activity*. Sometimes, a company decides to take a share in a business partnership instead of running the entire business itself. What's reported here is only the amount Amazon is entitled to, and it's not particularly significant.

Subtract the *tax* and *equity-method investment* from the operating profit, and you have *net income* or profit. And, this is "the bottom line".

But as a shareholder, you haven't quite got everything you need from the income statement yet. You may want to know how much of this net income your handful of Amazon shares entitles you to. For instance, if Amazon had doubled the number of shares in the year, then although net income as a whole has gone up, you'd actually get a smaller share-out. So, you need to work out net earnings per share. (Actually, you don't, because Amazon has done it for you.)

But there are two kinds of earnings per share! *Basic earnings per share* is calculated on the average shares in issue during the period. So, for instance, if a share was issued at the beginning of October, it would only get one quarter's earnings (from when it was issued in October, to the end of the year in December). That's reflected by *weighing* that share as a quarter (1/4) of a share when calculating the basic earnings per share.

But many companies also issue stock options to their executives and to other staff, or might issue shares to pay for acquisitions, with a second slice payable after a year. So, you have shares overhanging - they'll be issued some time, but they haven't been issued yet. Those shares are taken into account with the *diluted earnings per share*. That's the number we really want to look at.

Suppose a company doubled its revenues and profits by purchasing another company, and it did so in return for a small payment, but with the promise of a payment of shares after a year. (To make things easy, I'm also going to assume the company isn't growing.) Suppose that this would actually double the number of shares. If you looked at basic income, it would double this year and then halve next year. It would double this year because all the extra income is being divided between the same number of shares, and then it would halve next year as the new shares were issued.

Diluted earnings per share this year, on the other hand, would adjust for the new share issue. So, you would see earnings exactly the same next year.

It's not a realistic example, but it shows you how these things work!

(By the way, if a company splits its stock, by giving everyone five shares for every one, for instance, all the historic figures are restated. Stock splits often happen when the shares have gotten too expensive, so that instead of a stock being worth $5,000, shareholders get ten shares at $500 instead. A stock split happens when a company increases the number of its shares to boost the stock's liquidity.)

Example: Accrual system of accounting

The income statement isn't about cash going in and out. To explain how accruals work, it might be best to take a simple business example of two kids deciding to set up a lemonade stall.

They both take $10 each out of their piggy banks, and borrow the same amount of $10 interest-free from their parents. That's the starting capital - $20 equity, and $20 debt.

Then they buy a table and tablecloth for $20 and lemonade for $20.

They sell all the lemonade for $45 cash. How much money have they made this week?

Assuming they'll carry on with this lucrative business as long as the sun keeps shining, the table and tablecloth are a capital expense (that is, an investment in the business for the long term). Maybe they expect them to be useful for the whole 10 weeks of the season. This week, they'll only pay for 1/10 of the kit - $2 (that is, $20 / 10 weeks).

On the other hand, the lemonade has all been used up this week, so the full cost of that is taken.

That makes the profit $45 sales, less $20 cost of sales, less a $2 a week charge for the kit (which is called *depreciation*) - a grand total of $23 profit.

If you look at cash flow, though, they've paid out $40, and got back $45. Cash flow generated was just $5.

That, in a nutshell, is the accrual system - spreading sales and costs over the period that they cover - in this case for 10 weeks.

Balance Sheet

This is the next statement to look at. It shows what Amazon owns and owes, and it's on page 41 of the annual report. Here, we've only got two years of figures, not three.

While the income statement shows what Amazon earned over the whole period of the year, the balance sheet is a snapshot taken on 31st December. It's a single moment of the company's assets (things it owns) and liabilities (amounts that it owes) frozen in time. That's why, when I start talking about balance sheet ratios, you'll see that many of them use *averages* for the balance sheet numbers.

Take a look at the Amazon Consolidated Balance Sheet in 2020 example on the next page.

AMAZON.COM, INC.

CONSOLIDATED BALANCE SHEETS

(in millions, except per share data)

	December 31,	
	2019	2020
ASSETS		
Current assets:		
Cash and cash equivalents	$ 36,092	$ 42,122
Marketable securities	18,929	42,274
Inventories	20,497	23,795
Accounts receivable, net and other	20,816	24,542
Total current assets	96,334	132,733
Property and equipment, net	72,705	113,114
Operating leases	25,141	37,553
Goodwill	14,754	15,017
Other assets	16,314	22,778
Total assets	$ 225,248	$ 321,195
LIABILITIES AND STOCKHOLDERS' EQUITY		
Current liabilities:		
Accounts payable	$ 47,183	$ 72,539
Accrued expenses and other	32,439	44,138
Unearned revenue	8,190	9,708
Total current liabilities	87,812	126,385
Long-term lease liabilities	39,791	52,573
Long-term debt	23,414	31,816
Other long-term liabilities	12,171	17,017
Commitments and contingencies (Note 7)		
Stockholders' equity:		
Preferred stock, $0.01 par value:		
Authorized shares — 500		
Issued and outstanding shares — none	---	---
Common stock, $0.01 par value:		
Authorized shares — 5,000		
Issued shares — 521 and 527		
Outstanding shares — 498 and 503	5	5
Treasury stock, at cost	(1,837)	(1,837)
Additional paid-in capital	33,658	42,865
Accumulated other comprehensive income (loss)	(986)	(180)
Retained earnings	31,220	52,551
Total stockholders' equity	62,060	93,404
Total liabilities and stockholders' equity	$ 225,248	$ 321,195

Look for the figures that have <u>double underlines</u>.

There are two of them; one represents *total assets*, and the other is *total liabilities and stockholders' equity*. What do you notice about the figures?

Yup, they're the same, and they balance, which is why this is called a **balance sheet**.

It might be easier if you imagine the assets on one page and the liabilities on the facing page, instead of one on top of the other. They would then balance.

Let's go back to the lemonade stall and work out how balance sheets operate.

At the beginning of the week, the two kids have $20 of their own money (stockholders' equity) and $20 borrowed from the Bank of mum and dad (long-term debt). That's the *liability and stockholders' equity* side.

And at the beginning of the week, it sits opposite $40 of cash in the *asset* side.

At the end of the week, they have a table and tablecloth worth $20, less the $2 depreciation charge for the week.

They have sold out of lemonade, and they have $23 in profit, and $45 in the cash box (what they got from selling all the lemonade).

This is how the balance sheet changes;

- On the *asset* side, they now have equipment worth $18 ($20 − $2) and $45 in cash - that's $63.
- And as *liabilities and equity*, they still have the original $20 stock and $20 loans, but they have added another item, retained profit of $23. Which is also $63; hence it balances.

They have grown the total value of the business. But who benefits - them, or Mum and Dad? They do, because if we split down the liabilities and equity, the retained profit is part of the equity. They can either keep it on the balance sheet, or they can decide to pay themselves a dividend out of it. I would like to think these kids are smart enough to reinvest the money and sell even more lemonade next week!

Now with that out of the way, let's tackle the Amazon balance sheet, which, as you might imagine, is quite a bit more complex than the lemonade example above.

The assets start with *current assets* - that is, assets that are expected to be used up in less than 12 months. These are also assets that are liquid. That is, Amazon could get money for them in a short amount of time.

Cash and cash equivalents are fairly obvious.

Marketable securities include any investments such as a bond or stock, but not cash - basically anything that can be sold on the stock market.

Inventories would be items that are fairly easy to sell and probably turn over several times a year. So, if you're a retailer, you buy stock, and you expect to sell it pretty easily and quickly. For instance, if you're a fashion retailer, you expect to sell all your winter clothes, then your summer collection, then the fall collection... you get through three or four loads of different stock a year.

And *accounts receivable* represent sums other people owe Amazon and presumably will be repaid in the short term. (If you send goods by post with an invoice, and your year end comes before the money comes in, you have a receivable. That is because the customer would have to pay for the goods in the next accounting period. If the money comes in before the year end, you have cash.)

Current assets account for a little over a third of Amazon's assets. (That is $131,733m current assets in 2020, in comparison to total assets of $321,195m in 2020.) The rest are long-term assets.

The big item here is *property and equipment*. That includes all types of assets that support the business in the long term; warehouses, office buildings, computers, vehicles, conveyor belts, robotic systems, etc. I'm just looking at property and equipment here, and I think Amazon must have made relatively large investments in 2020. That's a thought we might remember for later when we look at the cash flow account. Remember that this number is a historic number. When Amazon buys a property, it's recorded in the balance sheet at what was paid for it, *less* depreciation, so it gets smaller over time.

Of course, in the real world, real estate generally increases in value. With most companies, it's not a big deal, but with older companies, you may sometimes find that there are significant assets that are worth more than is shown. For instance, a company may have an old factory site that is now in a residentially zoned area and worth far more to a residential developer than the value shown in the books. How do you find out? You have to read the notes *very* carefully - there's a note that tells you where the largest properties are.

Operating leases represent assets that the company leases rather than owns and probably cover similar types of assets.

Next is *goodwill*. This is a little bit more difficult to explain, but let me try. If you have a business and sell it, some of the money you get will pay for the assets in the business. But probably, you'll get paid more than just the liquidation value (net value of a company's physical assets if it were to go out of business and the assets sold) - you'll get paid for the business as a profit-generating enterprise. *So basically, the difference between the actual value of the assets and the price paid for the business is goodwill.* For example, if company A purchased company B for $5m, but the actual value of company B was $4.5m. In this case, company A has paid $500k as a Goodwill. Does that make sense?

Add in the *other asset*, and that's the total of the first side of the balance - *total assets*.

On the other side of the balance sheet, we have the liabilities and stockholders' equity.

In the *current liabilities*, again, the balance sheet starts out with the short-term stuff (i.e. within 12 months).

Accounts payable are amounts that Amazon owes to its suppliers. You might want to just note how they relate to inventories and accounts receivable. These three items together are called *working capital*, and they're quite important because they show how healthy the company's short term cash cycle is. Particularly with growing companies, you want to know that the working capital is being well controlled. I'll show you the ratios for checking that in the next chapter.

Next comes *accrued expenses*. These are expenses that you need to pay but haven't paid yet - such as unpaid vacation pay, utilities used but not paid for, and so on. They may also include tax for which the company has already incurred the liability but which will not need to be paid till sometime in the future - a deferred tax liability.

Unearned revenue is the other way round. If you have a subscription service, and the customer has paid you for 12 months but only used six, you have six months of unearned revenue. You have to carry on providing the service for the next six months.

All of these items make up *total current liabilities*.

But if you want to see how the company's long term funding is structured, you want to look at the long term liabilities. Basically, these split into two:

- equity, which is what the shareholders own, and
- debt, which is what the banks are owed.

You can treat long-term lease liabilities as debt because the company can't get out of them without repaying the amount it borrowed, and it has to pay interest on what's outstanding.

Long-term debt could be borrowings from banks or from the bond markets, which aren't repayable within 12 months, and on which the company has to pay interest.

Then we get to *stockholders' equity.*

The way it's displayed here is a bit over-complex for my needs; all I'm interested in is how much is 'original' capital, what stockholders paid the company for new stock, and how much is retained earnings. Basically, I want to see that the company has been adding a significant amount of retained income to what shareholders originally forked out. And yes, it has $52,551m retained earnings out of $93,404m total equity means well over half the equity has been added by the company and not subscribed by shareholders.

That's pretty much all you need to know about the balance sheet, but let's just think about different ways of balancing it. What you've got here is:

ASSETS = LIABILITIES + EQUITY

but you could also balance it differently, as:

ASSETS - LIABILITIES = EQUITY.

Don't trust me on this - do the sums, and check it out!

Cash Flow

People often talk about the cash flow statement as the third of the statements, but in the Amazon annual report it comes first, on page 38. It reconciles the numbers in the income statement with those in the balance sheet - so once you know your way around the math, you can always check that everything adds up. It also shows how much actual cash the company is generating. To do that, it strips out the accrual basis and only shows the movement of cash.

I particularly like the cash flow statement because the chances are, if a company tries to 'fix' its income statement by using aggressive accounting policies, it will show up in the cash flow. It will also show if a company is 'buying' its profits (that is, profits are growing, but the company is increasingly getting into debt).

The screenshot on the next page is from the Amazon Consolidated Statement of Cash Flows in 2020.

Fundamental Analysis for Beginners

AMAZON.COM, INC.
CONSOLIDATED STATEMENTS OF CASH FLOWS
(in millions)

	Year Ended December 31,		
	2018	2019	2020
CASH, CASH EQUIVALENTS, AND RESTRICTED CASH, BEGINNING OF PERIOD	$ 21,856	$ 32,173	$ 36,410
OPERATING ACTIVITIES:			
Net income	10,073	11,588	21,331
Adjustments to reconcile net income to net cash from operating activities:			
Depreciation and amortization of property and equipment and capitalized content costs, operating lease assets, and other	15,341	21,789	25,251
Stock-based compensation	5,418	6,864	9,208
Other operating expense (income), net	274	164	(71)
Other expense (income), net	219	(249)	(2,582)
Deferred income taxes	441	796	(554)
Changes in operating assets and liabilities:			
Inventories	(1,314)	(3,278)	(2,849)
Accounts receivable, net and other	(4,615)	(7,681)	(8,169)
Accounts payable	3,263	8,193	17,480
Accrued expenses and other	472	(1,383)	5,754
Unearned revenue	1,151	1,711	1,265
Net cash provided by (used in) operating activities	30,723	38,514	66,064
INVESTING ACTIVITIES:			
Purchases of property and equipment	(13,427)	(16,861)	(40,140)
Proceeds from property and equipment sales and incentives	2,104	4,172	5,096
Acquisitions, net of cash acquired, and other	(2,186)	(2,461)	(2,325)
Sales and maturities of marketable securities	8,240	22,681	50,237
Purchases of marketable securities	(7,100)	(31,812)	(72,479)
Net cash provided by (used in) investing activities	(12,369)	(24,281)	(59,611)
FINANCING ACTIVITIES:			
Proceeds from short-term debt, and other	886	1,402	6,796
Repayments of short-term debt, and other	(813)	(1,518)	(6,177)
Proceeds from long-term debt	182	871	10,525
Repayments of long-term debt	(155)	(1,166)	(1,553)
Principal repayments of finance leases	(7,449)	(9,628)	(10,642)
Principal repayments of financing obligations	(337)	(27)	(53)
Net cash provided by (used in) financing activities	(7,686)	(10,066)	(1,104)
Foreign currency effect on cash, cash equivalents, and restricted cash	(351)	70	618
Net increase (decrease) in cash, cash equivalents, and restricted cash	10,317	4,237	5,967
CASH, CASH EQUIVALENTS, AND RESTRICTED CASH, END OF PERIOD	$ 32,173	$ 36,410	$ 42,377

The first line shows *cash at the beginning* of the year. That's from the balance sheet, and what this account does is it shows the way cash came into and went out of the business during the year, which are all adjustments to the income statement. And then we'll finish up with the *cash at the end of the year*, the figure that goes in the balance sheet.

The balance sheet and cash flow figures for total cash don't quite agree. That's because the balance sheet excludes what's called restricted cash, for instance where it's needed as security. The cash flow account includes it. There's a note explaining that in the accounts. But frankly, it's a small number here, so we don't need to worry too much about it. (The cash in cash flow is $36,410m, and cash in balance sheet is $36,092m.)

So, the *operating activities* starts with *net income* - the bottom line of the income statement.

Then the cash flow statement adjusts it for all the accruals, which is shown under *Adjustments to reconcile net income to net cash from operating activities*.

The biggest item is almost always *depreciation and amortization*. If you remember, we depreciated the table in the lemonade stand example by $2 each week to spread the cost out over the 10 week summer season. In the Amazon accounts, depreciation is quite a bit more than net income. (By the way, amortization is the same thing as depreciation, only when intangible assets like software are involved.)

The *other expenses* are less significant, though *stock-based compensation* is worth keeping an eye on. Sometimes companies ramp it up, and it can involve heavy shareholder dilution. So here, it's not an issue, but just make sure you spot it happening if it starts becoming one.

Then you see *changes in operating assets and liabilities*, which is a non-user-friendly way of saying 'Changes in working capital'. When you build up your inventories, or when you give a customer credit, you are tying up your cash, so any increase in inventories or accounts receivable has to be subtracted from net income to get to the cash flow (you are paying out of your own pocket basically).

On the other hand, *accrued expenses* and *accounts payable* can be added back in. We add back accrued expenses because we haven't actually handed over cash for them yet, and accounts payable because we haven't paid them yet. (Wow, what happened to accounts payable in 2020?)

When all these adjustments have been made, you get the net operating cash flow or *net cash provided by operating activities* (no one ever calls it that).

Amazon has generated three times more in cash than it makes in net income, and its cash flow has been growing fast (that is the net operating cash flow of $66,064m over net income of $21,331m).

But now you need to look at how much Amazon had to invest in getting there. So, the cash flow adjusts for *investing activities*.

These figures should explain the movement in long term assets on the balance sheet; *purchases of property and equipment*, for instance. Just as a quick check, $40,140m of cash was spent on property and equipment, and in the balance sheet, the difference between 2019 and 2020 property and equipment items is $40,409m. Near enough!

Amazon has sold a few bits and pieces too, but not much. It also spent $2,325m on *acquisitions*.

But look at the figures for 2020 of *sales and maturities of marketable securities* and *purchases of marketable securities* - they're fairly chunky. In fact, when I looked up what was happening, it seems Amazon has been managing its treasury operations by buying a lot of short term government debt and other bonds, which is really cash management, not investment. Treasury operations are managing the company's cash and debt effectively - it's quite a niche element of head office finance.

So, for instance, a company will try to make sure its debt is secured for as long as possible at as low an interest rate as possible, and if it has cash on hand, it will invest it in short term bonds rather than leaving it in the bank, to make that little bit extra in interest. But if Amazon was buying stakes in other companies, that would probably have been for other reasons, like it wanted to support a small company that had technology useful to Amazon's operations or it wanted to lay the foundations for an eventual takeover.

At the bottom, you can see how much Amazon has invested each year under *net cash provided by investing activities*. It's a negative item, but it's still less than Amazon is generating from operating activities. However, the two lines of *net operating activities* and *net investing activities* have been getting closer together. So, I am going to want to find out what that big splurge of spending on capital and equipment was in 2020 and see what happens next.

Sometimes, companies invest much more in one year than they generate in cash. That's often the case with start-ups, and it can happen with companies that want to make a step-change. For instance, when software companies decided to switch from selling software licenses to selling Software As A Service, they often had to make huge investments in plant and equipment to support their cloud services. They then collect the benefits over the next several years. It can also happen with cyclical companies like automakers and chemical companies; they have to invest in big chunks.

But is that the case here? Or is Amazon spending too much? That's another thing I'm going to make a note of, to take a good look at.

The last set of cash flow items is cash flow from *financing activities*.

You can see here whether Amazon is borrowing more money or repaying debt; you'd also see here if it has issued any new shares. I'd be worried if I saw big numbers of new loans coming in. As it is, Amazon seems to be repaying its finance leases and has been repaying debt most years. That's a pretty solid performance, and if 2020 looks different, it's still not a huge change.

As you can see, before we start working out any of the ratios, I've already identified a few things I want to think about.

By the way, one number that's not shown here but that many analysts like to use is EBITDA (earnings before interest, tax, depreciation and amortization). It adjusts operating profit, or EBIT (earnings before interest and tax), but adds back *depreciation and amortization* - the big non-cash item, to get what you could call 'cash operating earnings'. It's a quick and dirty addition that you can do very easily, and it will come in useful later when we come to do valuations.

Normalizing earnings

With some companies, though not with Amazon, you may find that there's a big spanner in the works. For instance, a company might have discontinued a loss-making line of business, which - with the closure of businesses, write-off of obsolete stock, and write-off of all the equipment used in the business - creating a huge negative item. Or a company might have sold its old headquarters building to a real estate developer, making a huge profit, but obviously, not one that you'd expect to happen ever again.

Whatever the treatment of such sums by the accountants, as a fundamental analyst, you'll want to put a barrier on them and try to work out what are the underlying earnings. Most analysts do this, but it can create problems when looking at an adjusted figure from the analyst and an un-adjusted number from the company.

The most important thing is that you understand the impacts on the numbers and can detect the underlying trend.

You might want to adjust some other figures, too. For instance, if the company has a huge pension liability, it won't show that on the balance sheet, but you might decide that the value of the company should be shown adjusted for the pension's black hole. So, you would take the balance sheet total and subtract the pension liability, and then you would restate book value per share to take account of the liability.

You're restating book value per share so that you can see what the company's assets are worth if it has to pay the pensions liability first. That's being pessimistic. In the same way, if a company had a big lawsuit hanging over it, you might restate its net worth as if it had lost the lawsuit, and that gives you a bottom dollar figure for what it's worth - if the share price is less than that, it's safe to buy.

If you'd done that, you wouldn't have bought General Motors (GM) in the early years of the century; it had a negative net worth when restated. You also wouldn't have been surprised when GM filed for bankruptcy in 2005.

But that's not all!

While any analysis of a company and its stock will start with these three statements, you'll need to look further to make sense of the numbers. For instance, in Part I of the Annual Report, you'll find a description of the business and risk factors that could affect it. There's also a pretty brief recap of financial data for the past five years, which shows just headline figures, but gives you a good feel for the medium term performance of the company.

Looking at the notes in that table gives you two useful tidbits of information; first, that Amazon acquired Whole Foods in mid-2017, and secondly, that the account presentation of operating leases was changed in 2019. So, you might want to follow those up and see what difference those facts made to the numbers.

There's also a note on "Effects of COVID-19". You'll probably have guessed that lockdowns and customers' desire to avoid crowded shops led to increased buying from Amazon. But it also had costs, and Amazon strips them out here; $11.5bn in 2020, $4bn in the last quarter. Now, if you remember, I wondered why Amazon had so much capital spending in 2020, and this is part of the answer, I would guess. It's also why Amazon may not have repaid debt as much as it usually does.

On page 25, there's a breakdown of net sales, continuing with a breakdown of operating income on page 26. Amazon breaks down its business into three parts: North America, International, and AWS - the Cloud business. It also shows you the growth rates and percentages, so you don't have to work them out for yourself.

AWS only accounted for 12% of total sales. However, it made up more than half the operating profit! Because of those extra COVID costs, Amazon's retail business didn't improve its profitability very much. In contrast, AWS shot up from $9,201m to $13,531m. If you thought you were buying a retail operation, you might want to think about what that means for your assessment of the company.

I hope you're now beginning to get an idea of how the numbers in the accounts can provoke questions that may (or may not) be answered by the management's discussion of operations or the notes to the accounts. That's really key to being a good analyst, being able to join the two up - and it's something you will gradually learn by experience.

The footnotes - the best bit!

Reading the footnotes is always enlightening. I won't go through the whole report line by line because that would be really boring, but here are a few interesting items.

- When vendors use the Fulfilled By Amazon service, they send their goods to an Amazon warehouse, but they retain ownership. This stock *doesn't* appear on Amazon's balance sheet. That means its inventory might appear quite a bit lower than for conventional retailers with the same level of sales.
- The notes on accounts receivable and inventory tell you what Amazon had to write off or provide against possible bad debt. Those notes, for some companies, will be the first sign that their product is getting behind the times or they're giving too much credit to low quality customers. But there doesn't seem to be a problem here.

- Software development costs are capitalized, that is, they're put on the balance sheet (as if they were a piece of equipment that had been bought) - but the number wasn't significant. Sometimes, companies capitalize on very large amounts of software development costs or even customer acquisition costs; in some cases, that makes them look profitable when in fact, they're not. Well, that's not a problem here.
- Amazon tells you its depreciation policies. For instance, servers are written off over four years, and heavy equipment over ten years. Again, sometimes companies use depreciation to pad their income statement - everything seems in line here, though Amazon has possibly benefited a little by extending the life of servers from three to four years from the start of 2020 (they'll incur less depreciation annually).
- Note 3, on property and equipment, shows that Amazon has a huge leap of $15,228m of construction in progress. That gives me a feeling that there's a good chunk of spending to come next year.
- Note 6, debt, shows the maturities of Amazon's debt - that is, when it has to repay the loans. There's a small amount that has to be repaid by 2022, but the average life of the remaining debt is more than 11 years, so there's no big repayment coming up (with other companies, sometimes this note makes very uncomfortable reading).
- Note 7 is interesting: commitments. It shows all the finance leases, rent agreements, and debt payments that need to be made over the next five years. Check with the balance sheet to see if Amazon has enough cash to pay, and check with the income statement to see if it's making enough profit. Do you see any problem? I don't.
- One thing I'm delighted to see is that under 'suppliers,' the company says "no vendor accounted for 10% or more of our purchases." It's not good news when a company is dependent on a single big supplier.
- 'Legal proceedings' is always an interesting note. There's quite a lot going on here, so it's something stockholders need to keep an eye on.

- Note 10, 'segment information', gives you even more information on the breakdown of Amazon's business. It breaks down sales through online and physical stores, third-party sellers, and subscription services and also breaks out three big overseas markets - Germany, UK and Japan.

You'll also find, on pages 36-37, a letter from the auditors. It's boring, which is the way we like it. If an auditor's letter ever mentions words such as "qualified" or "going concern", it's a sign that the accountants have real worries about the way things are going. In the case of a going concern qualification, they think the business might not be able to make it through the year without refinancing. Ernst & Young seem to have no big issues other than the difficulty of calculating Amazon's tax position.

So, just going through a single year's annual report without getting out a calculator or doing any work on the ratios, we already have some interesting facts and some questions to ask.

Do you think you now know more about Amazon than you did? I bet you do. Do you think you have enough to value the shares?

Well, that may have made you think. We haven't really got to that stage yet. So, we need to do a little more work!

P.S. Before we go onto looking at the ratios, if you are finding this book useful so far - I would really appreciate if you could spare 60 seconds and <u>write a brief review on Amazon</u> on how this book is helping you. It would mean the world to me to hear your feedback!

Chapter 4 Quiz

1.   Which of these is not an asset?
    a.   Goods for resale held in inventory
    b.   The headquarters building
    c.   A loan note the company issued in 2009
    d.   Money owed by a customer for goods sold by the company

2.   Which of these is not a liability?
    a.   The company's share capital
    b.   Long term debt
    c.   Cash
    d.   Overdraft

3.   Which of these is a non-cash item?
    a.   Depreciation
    b.   Capital expenditure
    c.   Change in inventories
    d.   Repayment of finance

4.   What is goodwill?
    a.   Amazon's chain of thrift shops
    b.   What you paid for a business
    c.   Anything you paid for a business more than the cost of its assets
    d.   A nice feeling

5.   What is 'diluted' income per share?
    a.   A dividend paid to stockholders who don't drink alcohol,
    b.   Income per share including all stock that is to be issued later,
    c.   Income per share less tax already paid,
    d.   A measure of cash flow

5

Chapter 5: Why adding two and two sometimes makes more than four

In this chapter, I'm going to take you through the kinds of ratios that you can calculate from the numbers shown in the annual report. These ratios compare one item in the accounts with another, giving us information on what's happening in the business. Think of the ratios as being like a stethoscope, ultrasound, X-rays - they can show you what's going on underneath the skin. It's a way of comparing two numbers to create additional information, such as "two and two makes five".

They also give you ways to conquer time and space. That is, ratios let you compare Amazon today with Amazon in 1997 or in 2010. And they let you compare Amazon with Alphabet, Walmart, or any other company you consider as its peer group.

Financial news items often don't contain any ratios at all. They just report numbers - IBM's profits were down, PepsiCo's shares were up.

You'll get a story that leads with "Such and such stock was up 3% today as earnings rose 5%."

But suppose you know that the company's revenues were up 20%, and the debt on its balance sheet increased from 40% to 60% of the total capitalization? Then the real story is actually this one: "The margins the company is making on its sales fell dramatically, and its debt ratio increased making it a riskier trade if interest rates rise." But you won't hear that on CNBC.

What you're doing with ratios is comparing the different numbers in the financial statement in a way that shows you how the business is performing. For instance, you might compare revenues and profits to see how well the company is turning each dollar of sales into profit; you might compare profits and interest payments to work out if the company can service its debt easily; you might look at inventory turnover to see whether it's moving its stock out of the warehouse.

If you have surprises, such a bad quarter, or a ratio that doesn't look right, try to find an explanation elsewhere. For instance, a bad quarter might involve:

- the beginning of a downturn - if sales, gross margin, operating margin, and accounts receivable are all down;
- a lot of sales made but to customers who haven't yet paid - if accounts receivable is high; that means next quarter should be back on track;
- a big step change in a single cost (which you can see easily and which might reflect investment in a new area of business), or all the costs rising significantly (which is more likely to be a control issue and suggests management has lost its way);
- settlement of a major lawsuit (which is a non-recurring item).

Doing all the ratios properly and reading the annual report in detail will let you know which of these is the case. On the other hand, if you just look at the bare bones account in the newspapers, you won't be able to tell.

Every analyst has their favorite ratios. No single ratio on its own is going to tell you the whole story, but once you've worked out a number of them, you'll see how they relate, and you'll be able to use them just the way a detective uses clues.

Ratios can analyze current trends, the company's operations, its long-term investment in productive capacity, its financing, and its valuation. I'll show you each of these areas in turn. And again, I'll be using Amazon's 2020 financial statements.

Dear readers, if you want the full calculation breakdown of each ratio discussed in this chapter, please check the end of the chapter on page 125 as I have compiled together all the ratios and their calculations.

Trends

First of all, work out the trends in revenue, costs, and cash flow. You've probably done some of it already in the back of your head as you looked at the numbers in the last chapter. Now, calculate the percentage changes - what mathematicians call delta (Δ), but there's no great mystery in how to do it.

The table below shows Amazon's total net sales for periods 2018 – 2020.

	2018	2019	2020
Total net sales	$232,887m	$280,522m	$386,064m

So, Amazon's total net sales grew how much in 2019? And in 2020?

Simply take the difference between the 2020 and 2019 numbers; then work out the difference / 2019 number x 100, and you have the percentage.

And then do the same for 2019 and 2018 figures to get 2019's growth rate.

You should have 20.4% for the first year, and 37.6% for the second. That's a big increase!

The calculations are ($280,522m - $232,887m) / $232,887m x 100 = **20.4%**, and ($386,064m - $280,522m) / $280,522m x 100 = **37.6%.**

You can do the same for any of the figures in the report. And you can check trends against other trends. For instance, if sales are rising at a steady 15%, then accounts receivable should also be rising around that level, as should the Cost of Goods Sold and inventories. There might be a little difference, but there shouldn't be a major one.

Looking at trends is really interesting when you consider GameStop (GME). GameStop is a videogames and wargaming retailer. In its 10-K, it refers to this as an "intensely competitive industry" and also warns that gamers are increasingly downloading games direct rather than going to buy a DVD from a shop. Let's see how this plays out in the trends, using the selected financial info from the 10-K.

The table below shows GameStop's sales and growth rate for periods 2016 – 2020

	2016	**2017**	**2018**	**2019**	**2020**
Sales	$7,965m	$8,547m	$8,285m	$6,466m	$5,090m
Growth		7.3%	-3.1%	-21.2%	-21.3%

Okay, 2020 was affected by the pandemic. But 2019 was already looking bad. This company has been ex-growth for a while. Now let's look at the net income trend for GameStop in 2016 - 2020.

	2016	2017	2018	2019	2020
Net income	$305m	$230m	$-795m	$-464m	$-214m
Growth		-24%	n/a	-42%	-54%

I'm not getting a clear picture other than that this company has had either declining or negative profitability for five years. True, losses are declining. At the current rate, you'd feel the business will lose about $100m in 2021, half what it lost in 2020. (The 2021 results weren't out when I wrote this, but the consensus is that part way through 2022 it's just on the verge of breakeven.)

Also, 2018 growth is n/a because you can't work out a % change with one negative and one positive number.

I'm going to look at two other trends for GameStop. Let's put them both in the same table: dividends, and a statistic that's important for all retailers, same-store sales. (GameStop has recently been closing stores at quite a pace, so you'd expect same-store sales might go up if it closed the worst stores, which would be a reasonable expectation.)

Again, these stats are straight out of the 10-K, so you can go check them in their SEC Filings if you like.

The table below shows GameStop's dividend growth and same store sales for periods 2016 – 2020.

	2016	2017	2018	2019	2020
Dividend	1.48	1.52	1.52	0.38	0
Same store sales	-11%	+5.8%	-0.3%	-19.4%	-9.5%

What you see with the dividend is the first 3 years show the kind of progress you'd expect of a company in a mature industry sector with a stable business that's not growing fast. Then suddenly, the dividend gets cut to almost nothing, and then it's gone. That says management doesn't believe the problems are over. It's no longer trying to maintain the dividend, as it did in 2018 despite the poor results. It's in trouble, and it knows it.

And same store sales? Falling all the time since 2017.

Seeing this, there's no way I would have joined the Reddit WallStreetBets group in buying the stock. No way at all. They put on a classic short squeeze - hurting the hedge funds who had sold the stock short (selling without owning the stock) - and saw the price soar from below $20 to over $300. It's still sitting over $90 as I write this.

The underlying business hasn't changed, but GameStop's management are smart. They issued shares to take advantage of the high share price, so they now have $1.5bn more cash - they cleaned up the balance sheet nicely and that cash now accounts for about $13.6 a share.

So, to help you understand how I calculated the $13.6 per share, I looked through the financial report, on the company's website to find;

The cash in Q1 2022 was $1,035m.

Shares in issue 75.9m.

So, $1,035m / 75.9m = $13.6 cash per share.

 I still don't think the rest of the business is worth the remaining $76.40.

A philosophical note: you could say I'm dumb, and I missed a fantastic opportunity to make money. However, what about the guys who got in a little late and bought GameStop at over $300? They've lost two-thirds of what they put in. Fundamental analysis will sometimes mean you don't benefit from a big stock market movement - but it will stop you from buying trash that glitters but isn't gold.

Operations

These ratios are going to tell you how well the company is working on a day-to-day basis in running the business and serving the needs of its customers. The first set of ratios you'll want to look at comes from the income statement: different types of **margins**.

First of all, I want to calculate Amazon's *gross margin*. This is sales *less* cost of sales. For retailers, it's one of the most important ratios. Some retailers tell you exactly what it is, but Amazon doesn't. You have to calculate the gross profit first. So, looking at 2020, the total net sales is $386,064m *minus* cost of sales which is $233,307m, and that gives us $152,757m gross profit.

Gross margin is gross profit as a percentage of sales. That's *$152,757m / $386,064m x 100 = 39.57%*. You can calculate 2019 and 2021 yourself if you like. They don't look very different.

The next level of margin you want to look at is *operating margin*. This is a bit easier because Amazon gives you the operating income line; you don't have to calculate it. This comes in at *$22,899m / $386,064m x 100 = 5.93%*. That's actually higher than in either of the previous two years, so Amazon appears to be controlling costs well.

Remember that you need to have a feeling for the business behind the numbers. For instance, if you see a fall in margins, it could reflect a number of different factors, and your decision on whether to buy a company or not might be different, depending on the factors involved.

- Margins could have fallen because a company acquired a business that has lower margins, such as a distributor - a change in the *mix* of profits.
- Margins could have fallen because the product mix has changed. For instance, if consumers are buying more expensive meals as they feel more wealthy, a restaurant might see its margins increase markedly.
- Margins could have fallen because a company took over a lower-margin business that had been badly managed. In this case, you might expect better management to increase the margins over the next few years.
- Margins could have fallen because a company has decided to grab as much market share as possible from its competitors and is reducing prices to do so.
- Or margins might have fallen because management hasn't been controlling costs very well.

You won't know which of these explanations is right unless you read the words as well as the numbers!

Another figure I find quite helpful is tax as a percentage of profit before taxes. Here, it's 11.84% in 2020, against 16.98% in 2019 and 10.62% in 2018. That's all over the place. So that's something I would want to talk about with the company because I don't get a good feeling about what's normal and what tax rate is likely in the future. Remember, this figure is a provision - it's the tax that Amazon expects to pay, but it hasn't actually paid it yet.

In case you're wondering how I calculated tax rate of 11.84% in 2020...

Income before income taxes was $24,178m.

The provision for income taxes was $2,863m.

Tax rate = provision for income taxes / income before income taxes.

Tax rate = $2,863m / $24,178m x 100 = **11.84%.**

Another set of useful ratios are the *working capital turnover* ratios. These can show you how well the company is managing its current assets. Let's look first at *inventory turnover.* You can calculate the ratio quite simply, as inventory / cost of sales, for instance, but you can also calculate it in days - just multiply the number by 365. If a company has 30 days' inventory, that's not bad; if it has nearly a year's worth of inventory, that could be a problem.

Think about what this means. 30 days' inventory means I've sold all my stock in a month - if I was a store owner, I'd be pretty happy with that. But if I only trade my stock over once a year, I have all that money sitting in inventory in my store, and it's not selling.

Why do I use cost of sales, not sales? Because inventory will be in the books at what the company paid for it, not what it's sold for. Make sense?

Inventory turnover slowing down might mean the company has issues with outdated products. It might just mean management hadn't focused on inventory. Or it might involve a single bad decision; for instance, UK publisher Dorling Kindersley (DK) made a very bad decision on promoting the Star Wars franchise in 2000, pushing it to a £25m loss. (In fact, DK had other problems with its inventory; two months after it announced its results, it was bought out by Penguin books.)

The formulas for accounts receivable and accounts payable are similar. They both show you the amount of working capital in terms of the number of days of business that it supports.

Accounts receivable, the amount of credit given to customers, is calculated compared to revenues; it's sometimes called Days Sales Outstanding (DSO). Business to business (B2B) companies usually extend credit to their customers and DSO shows how good they are at getting paid on time.

Now, I'm going to introduce a little refinement here, because as you remember from the last chapter, the balance sheets show you snapshots at the beginning and the end of the period, while the income statement covers the whole year in between. So, you take the average value of accounts receivable over the year, rather than starting or ending balance. (That's simple to do - just add the starting and closing balance amounts together, then divide by two.)

So, can you do those ratios for Amazon? If you're struggling, check page 125.

As for accounts payable, this represents the amount of credit the company can get from its suppliers. You may think it's good that a business can get its suppliers to pay for its goods. Tour operators don't have to pay hotels till after their vacationers stay in the hotel, even though the customer has already paid for the vacation. That can give the operator significant amounts of credit from suppliers. However, not all businesses are like this. Sometimes, lengthening accounts payable can show the company has problems.

UK bookseller Pentos was a case in point - this is going way back to the 1990s before Amazon started challenging the bricks-and-mortar bookshops. Pentos bought many bookshops, including the famous Foyles on Charing Cross Road in London. It looked good on paper.

However, if you analyzed the annual reports, you would have seen its accounts payable increasing every year, way ahead of its sales. That meant it was getting its suppliers to pay for its business.

My friend's father knew someone who was working in a publishing house at the time, and he was getting a bit worried about Pentos not paying his bills when he sent them books. Fortunately, his dad mentioned it to his accountant. And his accountant said, "Look at the accounts payable. What's happening there?".

Well, his dad took a look at the annual report and saw what was happening to accounts payable. And then he phoned his friend who worked at the publishing house and explained what he'd found. And his friend decided not to do business with Pentos anymore.

6 months later, Pentos went bust. That was a good call!

Of course, you wouldn't normally want to buy or sell a share based purely on the accounts receivable ratio. But the story goes to show that spending quality time with a set of accounts can sometimes pay off in a surprisingly big way.

The ratios for Amazon's 2020 inventory turnover, accounts receivable and accounts payable are presented below.

Inventory turnover

Total inventory was $23,795m.

Cost of sales was $233,307m.

Inventory turnover = total inventory / cost of sales x 365 days

Inventory turnover = $23,795m / $233,307m x 365 = 37 days.

This means Amazon turns over its inventory in a little more than a month.

Accounts receivable / Days Sales Outstanding

Accounts receivable were $24,542m.

You already have the net sales figure of $386,064m.

Day Sales Outstanding = account receivables / total net sales x 365 days.

Day Sales Outstanding = $24,542m / $386,064m x 365 = 23 days.

Amazon gets paid in less than a month.

Accounts payable turnover

Accounts payable were $72,539m.

You already have the cost of sales figure of $233,307m.

Accounts payable turnover = accounts payable / cost of sales x 365 days.

Accounts payable turnover = $72,539m / $233,307m x 365 = 113 days.

Amazon gets four times more credit from its suppliers than it gives to its customers, which is 113 days in comparison to 23 days.

Long term investments

These ratios compare the income the company is generating to the assets it uses to create that income. It's a way of seeing whether the company has invested well in its business and is getting value out of its property and equipment.

Again, I prefer to use average values for the balance sheet data. But if for whatever reason the prior year's balance sheet is not available, then use what you have in the current year.

All of these ratios are slightly different in their exact significance. But don't sweat the small stuff here. All of them will give you good information.

Return on Invested Capital (ROIC) is calculated as *net operating profit after tax (NOPAT) / invested capital*; or you might like to work it out as *(net profit + dividends) / (debt + equity)*. This tells you how efficiently the company is investing its capital to generate positive returns.

If ROIC is less than the interest rate, or less than the company's cost of capital (WACC), then the company isn't getting a good enough return on its funds. On the other hand, a high ROIC suggests the company is successful in using its finance to generate returns, and might justify the company being re-rated (given a higher price/earnings ratio to reward its performance).

Return on Capital Employed (ROCE) is a slightly different look at efficiency, because it takes income before interest and tax (EBIT), and compares this to *total assets less current liabilities*. It gives us pretty much the same information as ROIC, just at a different level.

Return on Assets (ROA) looks instead at the return it makes on its total asset base. It is calculated as *net income / average total assets*.

These ratios work out the profitability of the company as a whole. But of course, if the company has long term debt, some of the returns will go to paying banks and bond interest. You want to know as a stockholder how good the returns are for you specifically. The ratio to find this out is **Return on Equity,** calculated as *net income / shareholders' equity*.

Okay, now let's calculate the ratios for Amazon!

ROIC

Total net income was $21,331m.

Invested capital is made up of equity $93,404m, long term debt $31,816m, and long term lease liabilities of $52,573m, which added together is $177,793m.

ROIC = total net income / invested capital

ROIC = $21,331m / $177,793m x 100 = 12%.

ROCE

EBIT was $22,899m

Total assets were $321,195m, while current liabilities were $126,385m. That gives us total assets *less* current liabilities of $194,810m.

ROCE = EBIT / (total assets - total liabilities).

ROCE = $22,899m / $194,810m x 100 = 11.75%.

ROA

Total net income was $21,331m.

Average total assets is calculated by adding the total asset figure at the beginning of the year (i.e. the end of 2019) and the end of the year (the 2020 figure), then dividing by two.

Total assets were $225,248m at the start of the year. And $321,195m at the end.

$321,195m + $225,248m / 2 = $273,221m.

ROA = total net income / average total assets

ROA = $21,331m / $273,221m x 100 = 7.8%.

ROE

Total net income was $21,331m and shareholders' equity $93,404m.

ROE = total net income / shareholders' equity

ROE = $21,331m / $93,404m x 100 = 22.84%.

Now, how can you use those ratios? First of all, you can compare companies with other similar companies and see which are doing better than the others. For instance, if you compared food processing companies, retailers, or video games publishers, you'd find that most of them had ratios that looked fairly similar across the sector, though they might be very different from other sectors like mining or energy. You can also see if a company has managed to improve the return on assets. For example, if a company is relatively new and has been spending money to develop a new product, that might have held returns back for a few years, but you'll see it improve as the new product gains success.

You should also consider what the company pays for its finance - **WACC**, the Weighted Average Cost of Capital. Although it's easy to think of equity as 'free', the company has to generate a certain amount of profit to keep stockholders from selling out, so there's a rate of return it needs to make for this purpose. It's usually calculated, and this gets complex, using the Beta (β), a measure of the share's volatility compared to the market (that is, whether it moves in step with the market, ranges much more widely, or moves less).

The formula is: *Risk-free rate + (Beta x [market rate of return - risk-free rate]).*

Or if you're a mathematical genius, you would be familiar with expressing it as:

$$E(R_i) = R_f + \beta_i(E(R_m) - R_f)$$

If an economist ever mentions CAPM (Capital Asset Pricing Model), that's the formula they mean! Basically, it's the same formula as WACC, but seen from another aspect. The required rate of return for it to be worth investing, given the risks.

You don't really need to know how to do this, as you can find WACC for most companies on the internet, but it's a good idea to understand it.

Taking it apart a piece at a time: the risk-free rate is usually the return on short term Treasury bills - the safest thing you can buy, or some people use 10 Year Treasuries. Short term Treasuries are safe because (1) they have U.S government backing, and (2) since they are short duration, there is not a big risk to the price if interest rates change, compared with longer term bonds.

Market return is the return for the whole stock market, so that's around 9%, according to global investment bank Goldman Sachs. If the stock is quite volatile, it might have a beta of 1.3 (according to Bloomberg).

So, I looked up the 10-year Treasuries today and got **1.92%** as the risk-free rate.

So, if we plot in the formula, we'd get 1.92 + (1.3 x [9 - 1.92]).

In simpler terms that's *1.92 + (1.3 x 7.08), or 1.92 + 9.204 = 11.12%.*

I hope that makes sense, but wow! That's a lot higher than you probably thought, am I right?

Most people think cost of capital is around the level of mortgage rates (2-3%), because they don't understand how much equity costs.

So, then you need to *weight* the cost of capital. That means looking at the mix of debt on the balance sheet and its average cost.

That's one reason the note on debt in the Amazon accounts shows so much detail - as well as the cost of equity.

So, then you work out:

- *debt / total liabilities as a percentage, multiplied by the cost of debt*
- *and equity / total liabilities as a percentage, multiplied by the cost of equity.*

Add the two together, and there you have the WACC.

Amazon's Debt/equity calculation

Total liabilities aren't shown as a figure on the balance sheet, so you need to add together the current liabilities of $126,385m, long term lease liabilities of $52,573m, long term debt of $31,816m, and other long term liabilities of $17,017m. That adds up to $227,791m. Equity is $93,404m, so you should get:

$227,791m / $93,404m = 2.43 (or 243% if you prefer to calculate the percentage).

But you could probably, as a shortcut, miss the beta part of the calculation to make life easier. It's not methodologically correct, but it's *good enough*.

Remember that one of the advantages you have over a stock market analyst is that you can take shortcuts if you need to...

I once looked at a company that some analysts highly rated only to find its return on capital was lower than keeping money in the bank. That didn't look like it was going to change in the medium term. What would you have done?

Well, I walked away. I decided my money would be better off staying in the bank till I found a better investment.

Financing

The next set of ratios tells us how well the company is managing its finances and its financial strength. Sometimes, this set of ratios warns me when a company's business isn't really sustainable, even though it looks quite good in terms of operational ratios.

These ratios involve the balance sheet. First of all, there's a very simple ratio that just looks at the liabilities side of the balance sheet and that's the **debt to equity ratio**.

The easiest way to calculate it is to take the total liabilities that aren't equity, and divide it by the equity; *Total Liability / Equity*.

It's a useful number, but you have to compare it to other companies in the sector, as the kind of ratio that a company can carry depends on its business model. For instance, REITs and subscription service companies can manage a high debt to equity ratio because their revenues are highly stable. The debt / equity ratio in the real estate sector is 352%. For food producers, it's just 79%.

One of the things the debt / equity ratio makes very clear is how many suppliers and lenders are in the queue ahead of you as a shareholder.

But I find the debt/equity ratio a bit unconvincing. Those liabilities include some things like deferred tax, which you wouldn't normally call 'debt'.

Also, companies sometimes have large amounts of cash, which I think needs to be set off against their debt. So, I prefer to calculate debt by taking the *cash, current debt, and long term debt*. And then I prefer to look at that compared to the balance sheet total as a whole. This is the **gearing** ratio - another percentage. It's a bit more difficult to calculate, as sometimes I need to delve into the notes to the accounts to get the right numbers.

Suppose the gearing ratio is over 100%. In that case, it tells me that the bankers are ahead of the stockholders in the queue for payment if anything goes wrong. Remember that the banks get paid first, so if debt is growing and equity isn't, that means the banks are more likely to get paid than you are.

By the way, remember when you're looking at stockholders' equity on the balance sheet that it doesn't relate to the price of the shares or how they trade in the secondary market. If I sell my shares in Amazon to you or a broker, that will not be reflected in the accounts. What's shown in the accounts is what Amazon received for new shares that they issued, most notably in the IPO.

Even if a company is well funded, life can get difficult if it doesn't manage its working capital well. If they don't manage to get customers to pay them on time but have to pay suppliers and banks in the meantime, things can get awkward. It's the corporate equivalent of realizing you have five more days till payday but you need to fill the tank with petrol and pay your home loan before then, and there's not enough money in the account. That happens, even if you're earning good money. And it can happen with companies, too.

The ratios for Amazon's debt/equity and gearing are presented below.

Debt/equity

Total liabilities isn't shown as a figure on the balance sheet, so you need to add together the current liabilities of $126,385m, long term lease liabilities of $52,573m, long term debt of $31,816m, and other long term liabilities of $17,017m. (Or you could simply deduct shareholder's equity from the liabilities and equity total.) That adds up to $227,791m.

Equity is $93,404m.

Debt/equity = Total debt / equity

Debt/equity = $227,791m / $93,404m = 2.43 (or 243% in percentages).

Gearing

Here again, you need to calculate a figure that's not shown on the balance sheet by taking the long term debt of $31,816m and subtracting the cash of $42,122m.

Oh, Amazon actually has more cash than debt!

Otherwise, you'd need to calculate long term debt / $93.404m equity.

Fortunately, you can work out a ratio that tells you if the company is likely to get caught with its pants down, so to speak. This is the **current ratio.** It's easy to calculate: *current assets divided by current liabilities (CA/CL).*

The higher the ratio, the better; the lower, the trickier. If a company has current assets several times its current liabilities, it should be able to find the money to pay its bills by selling off some inventory or getting a few customers to settle their bills.

Suppose it has lower current assets than current liabilities. In that case, it will not be able to cover its bills if it has to do so suddenly. It generally needs to be compared within a company's sector as different businesses have different cash flow characteristics, but if it is lower than the sector average without a good explanation, you might worry.

For Amazon in 2020, current assets are shown on the balance sheet as $132,733m, and current liabilities as $126,385m.

Current ratio = current assets / current liabilities

Current ratio = $132,733m / $126,385m = 1.05.

Retailers are between 1 and 1.5, so Amazon is towards the lower end. It's still above 1, but it might be worrying if it was below 1.

Some analysts also like to use the **quick ratio**. Instead of using current assets as a whole, it picks out just the following: *cash + cash equivalents + short term investments + accounts receivable.*

The argument for the quick ratio is that inventories might not be liquid. That is, the company couldn't easily turn them into cash in short order. This is usually the same as the **acid test** - *cash and accounts receivable divided by current liabilities.*

But suppose you were looking at a company where accounts receivable could take a long time to receive, for instance, in construction or in aerospace. In that case, you might also miss out on the accounts receivable.

If the quick ratio is less than 1, the company doesn't have enough liquid assets to meet its liabilities. That can be a problem. However, you need to consider the type of business. Retailers, for instance, get through inventory very fast, so their inventory is pretty close to cash - particularly with grocers, less so with white goods or fashion retailers. A retailer's acid test could look poor, but it's probably not a major problem if the current ratio is good.

Again, for Amazon in 2020, this is very similar to the current ratio, but we take out the inventories, which might not be sellable in time.

So liquid current assets are $132,733m less $23,795m, which is $108,938m.

Current liabilities are the same $126,385m.

Quick ratio = (current assets - inventories) / current liabilities

Quick ratio = $108,938m / $126,385m = 0.86.

Those ratios above just look at the balance sheet, but you can also look at whether paying debt services puts pressure on the company in terms of its income statement.

You might look at either **EBIT / interest payable**. Or you can look at **EBITDA / interest payable** (which removes depreciation and amortization).

For the EBIT version, 1.5 is a good healthy ratio; anything below that puts the company at risk of being unable to pay its debt servicing.

For Amazon in 2020, EBIT was $22,899m.

Net interest is made up of $1,647m interest expense, deducting $555m interest income, making a total of $1,092m net interest payable.

Interest cover = EBIT / net interest.

Interest cover = $22,899m / $1,092m = 20.9 times.

Amazon is unlikely to have problems paying its debt servicing, as its EBIT can cover it 20x times over.

A digression - catching out the creative accountants

It won't surprise you to know that companies are keen to push their earnings up as high as they can. Sometimes, the accountants decide to give reality a little help.

That can go all the way from adding a little sparkly eyeshadow to a beautiful set of accounts, to full-scale lipstick on a pig - except that you will need sharp eyes to spot the latter!

For instance, sometimes, sales can be artificially created. If you're desperate for revenue, you could pad out your accounts by making sales;

- to partners or affiliates - related party transactions,
- by bartering or promising to offset the cost against future sales,
- by offering large discounts for early booking.

So how can you catch the bad guys? For a start, if there are sales to partners or affiliates, the notes to the accounts will have to show *related party transactions* under the relevant note. I checked; there were many entries under this heading in the 2000 Enron report. Whether they would have been enough to put me off buying the stock, I don't know.

Secondly, if the company indulges in 'channel stuffing' to bring forward sales that would otherwise have fallen next quarter, you'll likely be able to tell because accounts receivable will be swollen. It's like that picture of when a python has eaten an elephant - the company hasn't got around to 'digesting' those extra sales. The ratios will help you here.

Companies can sometimes report artificially high profits for a long time by using aggressive accounting policies. For instance, start-ups sometimes capitalize a lot of their expenses, meaning they don't have to take their costs as an expense on the income statement. They sweep them under the carpet by putting them on the balance sheet and calling them "development" assets. You can check this by looking at the accounting policies and the long term assets for intangible assets; *look at the footnote and find out what they are.*

Amortizing assets too slowly is another way to boost profits. Again, look at the summary of accounting policies or the footnote on fixed assets.

If, for instance, Amazon had decided to amortize its real estate over 120 years instead of 40, it would have shrunk that cost by 1/3. That would be outrageous!

As you do your research, you'll get a feeling for each industry's norms on depreciation. A big paper-making machine will probably last 10-20 years; a server farm, because of the fast progress in technology, probably won't last so long.

Valuation ratios

When you calculate the ratios for Amazon, use the share price when the 2020 results came out: $3,292. That means you'll be seeing the ratios the way they actually were at the time, regardless of when you are reading this.

It might be interesting to think about the fairy tale of the Golden Goose in terms of valuation. The goose can lay 1 golden egg a day.

- As a bird for eating, she's worth about $12.
- A golden egg is worth about $2,500 (for one and a half ounces). So even if you just put off the roast goose till tomorrow, you've made a much bigger return.
- So that's $912,500 a year ($2,500, x 365 days). We're not looking at any growth here, though, just 365 eggs yearly.
- A domestic goose can live 20 years.
- So, the question is, how many years' worth of egg income do you want to pay for the bird? 20? She'll make the money back - but not anymore. And there's always the possibility of a revenue loss, for instance, if someone steals your goose.
- In any case, she *can't* be worth more than $18.25m (20 years x $912,500 a year).
- So now the question is, how much do you need to discount future years' cash flows back?

Perhaps the market values the goose at 12 years' revenue, that is, $10.95m ($912,500 x 12 years).

On the other hand, one analyst has seen the real money-making opportunity. If the chicks of the goose that lays the golden eggs can also lay golden eggs, you could have exponential growth… what would she be worth if you could breed her offspring and have 365 geese all laying golden eggs by the end of the year?

That was a bit of fun, but I hope it's made you think. It's also introduced you to the idea of valuation ratios.

The gold standard of valuation ratios that everyone uses is the Price/Earnings Ratio (or P/E ratio for short). It's really simple to calculate - *Price divided by earnings.*

So, a company with a share price of $528, and income per share of $30… you work it out!

… is selling on a P/E ratio of 17.6.

If you like to think of it this way, if you buy the shares, you are paying 17.6 years' earnings, so that's how long it will take for the company to earn its share price. Of course, you'd normally expect earnings to grow so that the payback would accelerate in future years.

As I write, the S&P 500 is trading at 25.78 times earnings, so 17.6 would be quite cheap compared to the market. But you would also want to compare the stock with other stocks in its sector, as valuations for different sectors can vary widely.

Amazon shows diluted net income per share of $41.83 at the bottom of their income statement for 2020.

If you used the $3,292 share price from the end of January 2021 when the report came out, you should have got:

P/E ratio = $3,292 / $41.83 = 78.6.

That's a very high valuation!

A.Z Penn

The table below shows you some of the highest and lowest valued sectors - software looks way high. The figure for air transport, though, is affected by the fact that the pandemic has depressed earnings, and no one really knows when the airlines will recover.

Sector	P/E ratio	Expected growth (next five years)
Banks	21.4	13%
Software	107.62	22%
Wireless telecom	76.82	19.5%
Air transport	7.4	45.6%
Building materials	34.82	17.9%

Source: Aswath Damodaran http://pages.stern.nyu.edu/~adamodar

By the way, do you remember we looked at the trends in GameStop's revenues, profits and dividends? Now, let's take a look at their valuation.

Analysts currently forecast that sales will continue to fall, but the company will make a profit in 2023 with a net income per share of $0.15.

Talking today's share price of $92.69, that gives us a price/earnings ratio of 617 ($92.69 / $0.15).

At the top of the boom, GameStop was trading on a two-years-in-the-future P/E ratio of 2,166.

Amazon is trading about 40 times year two forecasts.

And Amazon is one of the retailers that's taking shares away from GameStop. Which would you rather have in your portfolio?

Another option for a valuation ratio that was very popular in the tech boom is **price/EBITDA**. It's still a useful ratio, but I prefer to use it as a secondary ratio, putting the P/E ratio first.

The problem is that if you only concentrate on pre-interest and pre-tax earnings, you run the risk that once the bank has taken their cuts, there's nothing left for you as a shareholder. It can still give you some insights when you are comparing companies to each other.

For Amazon in 2020, EBITDA is calculating by operating income of $22,899m, together with the $25,251m of depreciation and amortization, which is shown on the cash flow statement. That's a total of $48,150m.

For price, you need to take the market capitalization of the company rather than the share price, so multiply the share price of $3,292 x 510 million shares, the amount shown at the bottom of the income statement. That gives you $1,678,920m.

Price / EBITDA = $1,678,920m / $48,150m = 34.8 times.

Obviously, it's less than the P/E ratio because EBITDA is more than net income - it's before a lot of costs get taken out like interest, taxation, depreciation and amortization.

Something I like to do with the P/E ratio is to turn it back to front and express it as **earnings yield**. (The mathematical term for a ratio turned back to front is the *inverse*.) The formula for that is simply *earnings per share / stock price x 100*.

For Amazon in 2020, diluted net income per share of $41.83 was shown in the income statements. And their share price was $3,292.

Therefore, earning yields is calculated as *$41.83 / $3,292 x 100 = 1.27%*.

I like earnings yield as a ratio. The price/earnings ratio doesn't easily compare with other investments. But you can directly compare the earnings yield as a percentage with returns on other investments, like interest rates on bonds or rental yields on real estate.

However, if you want to compare the dividend return on a stock to the return if you put the money in the bank, you'll want to look at **dividend yield**.

Amazon doesn't pay a dividend, so you don't need to calculate it.

However, if you were to buy REITs, real estate trusts which by law have to pay out a certain percentage of their rents in dividends, the yield would be one of the more important valuation ratios you'd want to know.

Let's look at Omega Healthcare Investors, ticker OHI. It's a REIT that owns elder care establishments and lets them out to assisted living operators.

The shares are trading at $27.62, and it pays a $2.68 dividend. The yield is $2.68 / $27.62 x 100 = 9.7%.

That's high, even for the REIT sector, which has an average yield around the 3.5% mark.

There are some concerns that OHI isn't well positioned - some of its major tenants are in financial trouble, and the elder care sector has done very badly in the pandemic, with occupancy levels declining markedly. OHI missed its Q4 forecasts, too. The dividend *might* be cut, but the company appears to have prioritized keeping investors on board so far. So, it's a higher risk, but potentially higher return investment than Realty Income (ticker O), one of the largest and best known REITs, which yields about 4%.

By the way, even if you're not a dividend investor, it's worth noting that dividends historically have accounted for more than a third of total equity returns.

How can you get a better idea of whether the OHI dividend is going to be paid? You can look at **dividend cover**. It's calculated as *net income per share / dividend per share*.

In the third quarter of 2020, for instance, OHI had $0.81 a share available for distribution and paid a dividend of $0.67, so the cover was 1.2 - safe, but only just. (This means the company is distributing the vast majority of its profits. If profits were to fall, it might have to cut the dividend. A company with higher dividend cover would be less likely to consider a dividend cut.)

REITs are a special case, by the way. They have a special tax break, in return for which they are legally bound to distribute a set percentage of their income. For other companies, dividends are entirely at management's discretion. Many, like Amazon, don't pay a dividend at all.

Price to book used to be a ratio that analysts loved. If you read any investment book written before about 1980, there will be a lot about the price to book in it. It's less important nowadays, and the technological revolution, along with the shift in the economy away from manufacturing and towards services, is a big reason.

Price to book can be very simply calculated - *market capitalization* (which is all the shares in the company at today's share price, usually shown on the summary page of financial websites) *divided by total stockholders' equity*.

So, for Amazon, as I write this the market cap is $1,678bn, and equity at the end of 2020 was $93.4bn. It's trading at 17.9 times its book value.

But there are two ways to calculate this.

You could either calculate shareholder's equity per share as $93,404m / 510m shares = $183, and compare that to the share price of $3,292:

$3,292 / $183 = 17.9 times.

Or you could calculate market capitalization to the total shareholders' equity of $93,404m: it's just the same (or should be if you've got it right).

510m x $3,292 = $1,678,920m (you already did that calculation once for market capitalization, remember?)

So, $1,678,920m / $93,404m = 17.9 times.

If you look up the works of great value investors of preceding generations, they liked to buy stocks at less than book value if they could. But they were buying railroads, aluminum smelters, and big auto factories - the kind of businesses with huge amounts tied up in plant and equipment. Even with its big logistics side, Amazon's business is far more biased towards the skills economy - creating its own software, algorithms, and marketing strategies. So, to conclude, price to book is not really such an important ratio these days.

Which earnings and which P/E ratio to use?

You may already have spotted an issue with the P/E ratio. If I use last year's earnings, they're already out of date; but if I use next year's forecast earnings, how good is the forecast?

Usually, I look at TTM - the 'trailing twelve-month' P/E ratio. This adds together the quarterly income per share for the last four quarters. Hence, it is only ever one quarter in arrears, not a whole year. Yahoo Finance and most other websites show it - though it's easy to calculate yourself, as long as you have the last four quarterly reports.

For fast growth companies, though, it's useful to forecast earnings and to look where the P/E ratio will be in two years' time. I'm just going to show you on the next page an example of a fast growth company against a mature company and how the P/E ratios work out.

	Last year	Year 1 forecast	Year 2 forecast
Mature company share price	$150	$150	$150
Earnings	$10	$11	$12
P/E ratio	15	13.6	12.5
Growth company share price	$300	$300	$300
Earnings	$10	$20	$30
P/E ratio	30	15	10

Although, right now, the growth company looks twice as expensive as mature company. If our year two forecasts are right, it will end up selling on a lower P/E ratio in two years' time.

Now, the keywords here are "if our year two forecasts are right".

During the tech boom, the forecasts ran away with themselves. And you can imagine, if a growth company disappoints and ends up just earning $12 instead of $30 in year 2, it will still be outrageously highly valued - or else, the share price will take a dive.

There is no 'right answer' here. But you have lots of tools for assessing both companies. The growth company might be a steal, or not.

There are two other tools can help you when you're thinking about P/E ratios. One is the long term average P/E ratio, for the market or for a stock. This takes past earnings and the share price when those earnings were announced. It's a bit of a hassle to calculate. Fortunately, for the S&P 500, you can get the long term average. I use a site called Macrotrends which lets me see it as a chart, but you can hover over any data point to see the value...

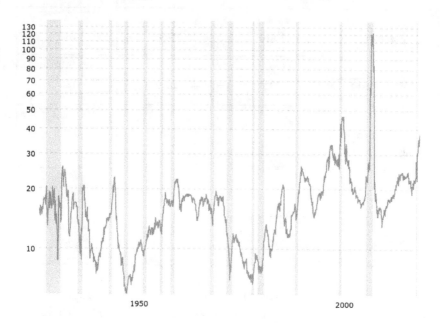

Wow! P/E ratios hit 120 in May 2009! On the other hand, in around 1980, you could have picked up the S&P 500 selling at just 7.5 times earnings, at the end of the decline that began with the early 1970s crash.

The second tool helps address the problem of whether a P/E ratio for a growth company is worth paying. It's called the **PEG ratio**, or *price earnings to growth*, and it tells you how much you're paying for each dollar of growth.

It's straightforward calculate too; *price earnings ratio / growth rate.*

Let's look at high-PE, high-growth stock Tesla (TSLA). It's on a P/E ratio of 188. And it's expected to more than double its earnings this year - 108% growth - and then to grow by 25% next year.

So, depending on which year we want to look at, the PEG could be 188 / 108 = 1.74 this year, or 188 / 25 = 7.52 next year.

I will quote Peter Lynch again because I think he often gets things right. He thinks that a good growth company should sell on a PEG of 1.0 - that is, the P/E ratio should be exactly the same as the expected earnings growth. If you can get it below 1.0, it's a bargain.

I have not found out what Lynch thinks about Tesla… but you can probably guess. I would think Lynch would have thought Tesla was heavily overvalued, and he might have it on a watch list in case the shares fell to where they represented fair value, though.

The numbers are never the whole story - but they are the clues. And like a good detective, if you follow up the clues, you'll find out what's really going on.

Chapter 5 Quiz

1. Which of these is *not* a reason that gross margins would increase?
    a. The company put prices up
    b. A major cost input became cheaper
    c. The company sacked half its head office team
    d. The mix of products sold changed

2. Working capital is made up of
    a. Inventories and accounts receivable
    b. Inventories and accounts payable
    c. Inventories and accounts receivable, less accounts payable
    d. Long term debt less short term assets

3. Why could return on assets increase?
    a. Profits increase on a stable asset base
    b. Interest rates go up
    c. The company launches a new product
    d. A long term loan becomes due

4. What is gearing?
    a. A measure of debt compared to equity finance
    b. The relationship of inventories to sales
    c. The Shimano ratio multiplied by the Sturmey Archer factor
    d. The speed of increase in sales

5. The earnings yield is ---- of the P/E ratio.
    a. The inverse of
    b. The opposite of
    c. Irrelevant to
    d. The same as

Answers to Amazon ratio calculations

As this is probably the first time you're going to be doing these calculations, I haven't just given the answers, but also the numbers found in the annual report for 2020, and the calculation that gives you the right number. (If Amazon's 2021, 2022, and 2023 reports have come out since this book was published, your next step is to grab those and do the same calculations till you find all of them easy to do.)

Gross margin

Total net sales were $386,064m in 2020.

Cost of sales was $233,307m.

Gross profit = net sales - cost of sales = $152,757m.

Gross margin = gross profit / total net sales x 100

Gross margin = $152,757m / $386,064m x 100 = 39.57%

Operating margin

You already have the net sales figure of $386,064m.

Operating income was $22,899m.

Operating margin = operating income / total net sales x 100

Operating margin = $22,899m / $386,064m x 100 = 5.93%

Tax rate

Income before income taxes was $24,178m.

The provision for income taxes was $2,863m.

Tax rate = provision for income taxes / income before income taxes.

Tax rate = $2,863m / $24,178m x 100 = 11.84%.

Inventory turnover

Total inventory was $23,795m.

Cost of sales was $233,307m.

Inventory turnover = total inventory / cost of sales x 365 days.

Inventory turnover = $23,795m / $233,307m x 365 = 37 days.

This means Amazon turns over its inventory in a little more than a month.

Accounts receivable / Days Sales Outstanding

Accounts receivable were $24,542m.

You already have the net sales figure of $386,064m.

Day Sales Outstanding = account receivables / total net sales x 365 days.

Day Sales Outstanding = $24,542m / $386,064m x 365 = 23 days.

Amazon gets paid in less than a month.

Accounts payable turnover

Accounts payable were $72,539m.

You already have the cost of sales figure of $233,307m.

Accounts payable turnover = accounts payable / cost of sales x 365 days.

Accounts payable turnover = $72,539m / $233,307m x 365 = 113 days.

Amazon gets four times more credit from its suppliers than it gives to its customers, which is 113 days in comparison to 23 days.

Return on Invested Capital (ROIC)

Total net income was $21,331m.

Invested capital is made up of equity $93,404m, long term debt $31,816m, and long term lease liabilities of $52,573m, which added together is $177,793m.

ROIC = total net income / invested capital.

ROIC = $21,331m / $177,793m x 100 = 12%.

Return on Capital Employed (ROCE)

EBIT was $22,899m

Total assets were $321,195m, while current liabilities were $126,385m. That gives us total assets *less* current liabilities of $194,810m.

ROCE = EBIT / (total assets - total liabilities).

$ROCE = \$22,899m / \$194,810m \times 100 = 11.75\%.$

Return on Assets (ROA)

Total net income was $21,331m.

Average total assets is calculated by adding the total asset figure at the beginning of the year (i.e. the end of 2019) and the end of the year (the 2020 figure), then dividing by two.

Total assets were $225,248m at the start of the year. And $321,195m at the end.

$321,195m + $225,248m / 2 = $273,221m.

ROA = total net income / average total assets.

$ROA = \$21,331m / \$273,221m \times 100 = 7.8\%.$

Return on Equity (ROE)

Total net income was $21,331m and shareholders' equity $93,404m.

ROE = total net income / shareholders' equity.

ROE = $21,331m / $93,404m × 100 = 22.84%.

Debt/equity

Total liabilities isn't shown as a figure on the balance sheet, so you need to add together the current liabilities of $126,385m, long term lease liabilities of $52,573m, long term debt of $31,816m, and other long term liabilities of $17,017m. (Or you could simply deduct shareholder's equity from the liabilities and equity total.) That adds up to $227,791m.

Equity is $93,404m.

Debt/equity = Total debt / equity.

Debt/equity = $227,791m / $93,404m = 2.43 (or 243% in percentages).

Gearing

Here again, you need to calculate a figure that's not shown on the balance sheet by taking the long term debt of $31,816m and subtracting the cash of $42,122m.

Oh, Amazon actually has more cash than debt!

Otherwise, you'd need to calculate long term debt / $93.404m equity.

Current ratio

Current assets are shown on the balance sheet as $132,733m, and current liabilities as $126,385m.

Current ratio = current assets / current liabilities.

Current ratio = $132,733m / $126,385m = 1.05.

Quick ratio/acid test

This is very similar to the current ratio, but we take out the inventories, which might not be saleable in time.

So liquid current assets are $132,733m less $23,795m, which is $108,938m.

Current liabilities are the same $126,385m.

Quick ratio = (current assets - inventories) / current liabilities.

Quick ratio = $108,938m / $126,385m = 0.86.

Interest cover

EBIT was $22,899m.

Net interest is made up of $1,647m interest expense, deducting $555m interest income, making a total of $1,092m net interest payable.

Interest cover = EBIT / net interest.

Interest cover = $22,899m / $1,092m = 20.9 times.

Amazon is unlikely to have problems paying its debt servicing, as its EBIT can cover it 20x times over.

Cash interest cover

EBITDA = operating income of $22,899m, together with the $25,251m of depreciation and amortization, which is shown on the cash flow statement. That's a total of $48,150m.

Interest payable = $1,092m.

Cash interest cover = EBITDA / interest payable.

Cash interest cover = $48,150m / $1,092m = 44 times.

Price/Earnings Ratio (P/E ratio)

Share price / earning per share.

Amazon shows diluted net income per share of $41.83 at the bottom of the income statement.

If you used the $3,292 share price from the end of January 2021 when the report came out, you should have got:

P/E ratio = $3,292 / $41.83 = 78.6.

That's a very high valuation.

Earnings yield

This uses the same data the other way round: *$41.83 / $3,292 x 100 = 1.27%.*

Earning per share / share price.

Price / EBITDA

EBITDA you worked out already (and if you've just been using a calculator, and not writing down your workings or using a spreadsheet, you've learned a lesson because you've got to recalculate it).

For price, you need to take the market capitalization of the company rather than the share price, so multiply the share price of $3,292 x 510 million shares, the amount shown at the bottom of the income statement. That gives you $1,678,920m.

Price / EBITDA = market capitalization / EBITDA.

Price / EBITDA = $1,678,920m / $48,150m = 31.8 times.

Obviously, it's less than the P/E ratio because EBITDA is more than net income - it's before a lot of costs get taken out like interest, taxation, depreciation and amortization.

Price to sales

Price to sales = market capitalization / total net sales.

Price to sales = $1,678,920m / $386,064m = 4.3 times.

Dividend yield

You don't really need to calculate this. As of today's date, Amazon had never paid a dividend.

But the formula is the annual dividend per year / share price.

Dividend cover

Nor does it need to be calculated here.

But the formula is: earning per share / dividend per share.

Price to book

There are two ways to calculate this.

You could either calculate shareholder's equity per share as $93,404m / 510 million shares = $183, and compare that to the share price of $3,292:

$3,292 / $183 = 17.9 times.

Or you could calculate market capitalization to the total shareholders' equity of $93,404m: it's just the same (or should be if you've got it right).

510m x $3,292 = $1,678,920m (you already did that calculation once for market capitalization, remember?)

So, $1,678,920m / $93,404m = 17.9 times.

Price/earnings-to-growth ratio (PEG ratio)

You already calculated the P/E ratio as 78.6, which was very high.

But the growth rate for 2020 was high, too.

Diluted net income per share grew from $23.01 to $41.83 - that's an 81.8% growth.

So the PEG is 78.9 / 81.8 = 0.96.

It's just below 1, which means you're paying less than a dollar for every dollar of growth.

However, what you need to know is whether that level of growth is going to continue. Was it a fluke?

6

Chapter 6: Industry fundamentals

Industry fundamentals are often overlooked by the 'pure mathematicians' in investment circles, but you can't do without understanding the industry. Numbers don't tell you anything unless you understand the business. For instance, here's a list of companies you might have thought were quite secure at one point:

- Blackberry
- Nokia
- Kodak
- Polaroid
- Blockbuster
- IBM.

Blackberry and Nokia missed a step in their markets. Blackberry is now a cybersecurity company, but its shares are currently listed at $7, way down from their $131 high; Nokia was acquired by Microsoft.

Kodak was way too late realizing what the digital revolution would do to its film sales, and filed for Chapter 11 bankruptcy in 2012.

Polaroid had already filed for bankruptcy much earlier, in 2001, facing a decline in the photography market.

Blockbuster saw video rental replaced by streaming and on-demand video services, and filed for bankruptcy in 2010: Netflix (which Blockbuster didn't think was worth acquiring!) ate its lunch and dominated.

As for IBM... it's currently reinventing itself as a power in hybrid Cloud, and despite some significant missteps on the way, it looks as if new CEO Arvind Krishna just might pull the rabbit out of the hat by surprising us all.

What all those companies have in common is that their markets were completely disrupted by new technologies. If you didn't understand the digital camera, or you didn't understand what was happening to the smartphone, or how cloud computing was changing the way enterprises structured their IT infrastructure, the numbers might have conned you into thinking things were okay.

In fact, sometimes the numbers look bad when companies are getting things right. Over the transition to SaaS (Software as a Service), companies were faced with a horrible dilemma. They would be cannibalizing their own revenues if they moved to a subscription model, selling a $100 a year subscription instead of a $600 software license.

What was good about the new model was that the quality of earnings was much better. So was cash generation. But the move from the old to the new business model was still a tough one.

Another thing you will need to know about a company is whether it has barriers to entry - what Warren Buffett calls 'moats'.

For instance, as a small landlord, I wouldn't have a big advantage over anyone else; but if I owned the biggest purpose-built student accommodation in a university town, I'd have a huge advantage over people who were just letting out a couple of rooms in a house. Companies with great moats might include:

- Amazon, naturally!
- Taiwan Semiconductor
- Baidu - "China's Google"
- PepsiCo and Coca-Cola, together, own the soft drinks business
- Novo Nordisk - leader in diabetes medication
- ADP - dominant provider of payroll services
- Slack - the network everyone uses to work, just acquired by Salesforce.

Additionally, I loved Slack's ticker - WORK.

A moat should be difficult for a competitor to fill in. It should also give the company pricing power because customers want the brand as they are locked into using the product. And it should keep ROCE/ROA higher than at companies which don't have moats (so check those ratios again).

You'll also want to understand the different cost inputs. Airline stocks got a double hit over the pandemic - first of all, they got ruined when passengers stopped flying, then they got hit all over again when oil prices rose.

You certainly want to know the company's market share in fragmented sectors like real estate because it can be difficult to ascertain. I always like to see 40-50%, but my feeling is that market share above 50% can be a mixed blessing or even a curse. A company with high market share is likely to draw the attention of the authorities - for instance, it may not have a free hand in setting its prices or may not be allowed to make what would otherwise be an attractive acquisition.

Also, in companies with high market share, sometimes the company starts to prioritize market share instead of profitability. For instance, management will decide not to raise the price of its most popular product in case it loses market share, when in fact, it is becoming less profitable all the time.

It is also worth noting that market share, by definition, can only add up to 100%. Sometimes, you'll find the top four companies in a niche all claim more than 25% of it. (In the internet boom, some companies stated growth rates that would have given them a 125% market share in five years.) Check what you think the whole market might be worth - see if there are any figures available from Gartner or one of the other IT research houses, for instance. Then see how much share that company is really likely to gain.

For some companies, such as retailers and restaurant chains, a map is a useful thing to have. You can easily see where the chain has room to grow. Moving into a different country or a different area can be risky - what works in the American Midwest doesn't always play in California - but if, say, you see that the company can easily open new outlets in its existing markets without saturating them, it has room to grow without major risks.

On the other hand, it was obvious when people started complaining about two Starbucks opposite each other on the same block that there wasn't much room for growth in the U.S - where it cut a large number of branches in 2008 and 2009. (Since then, though, it has grown internationally, keeping the share price moving upwards.)

A.Z Penn

Mergers, acquisitions and disposals

The big question with any corporate deal is: "Is this a good deal?" That's not just about the price paid but about why the acquisition is being made.

For instance, a company could acquire up or down its value chain to capture more of the value in its business by buying a distributor or supplier. This can sometimes be an excellent deal, particularly where access to particular customers or cost inputs is difficult. This is a type of *backward integration* - in fact, Amazon did this organically. As a retailer, it relied on publishers to supply it with books, but it began to allow authors to self-publish and create content on Amazon as well.

A company might acquire a competitor in order to gain economies of scale, or perhaps in order to have a low-end as well as a high-end product. *Consolidation* strategies are often used in fragmented sectors. However, they don't always produce value.

Waste Management Inc made over 100 acquisitions from 1968 to 1972, but it appears to have increased the size of its problems as well as the size of the company.

Some basic checks on the business

I always like to carry out some basic checks on the business. It's not at all a bad idea if you create a template for analyzing companies with the major headings printed out and fill a copy in every time you look at a new company. Yes, we have computers, but I like to do mine by hand, as I find it concentrates the mind.

- Add up the different bits of the business - do they add up to 100%, or is there a big 'other' item that isn't accounted for? Some companies hide a lot of failed business ventures in that 'other' space, and it can be worrying when you find out just what is in there.

- Try to find out the major suppliers. Find out how concentrated the market is; for instance, airlines pretty much have a choice of either Airbus or Boeing when they're buying their airplanes, so unless they are both large and prominent, they're unlikely to get a great price. On the other hand, major grocery chains are in a huge position of power compared to many food producers.

- Who are the customers? Try to segment the consumer market - this can be useful. For instance, when you look at Meta (formerly Facebook), one of the major issues it faces now is that younger people, who were originally responsible for the growth of the company, now prefer TikTok.

- Does the company suffer from customer concentration? For instance, some REITs only have four or five large tenants; some food companies only sell through two grocery chains. If one of those major customers stops renting the space or taking the product, for whatever reason, the company is going to have a hard time replacing the business.

- Get a good sense of the cash flow. How quickly does the company turn products or services into cash? How regular or lumpy is cash flow? How much credit does the company need to offer? Does the company have significant up-front costs like pitch costs when it's bidding for contracts?

- It's also really useful to check out the credit ratings of big customers and suppliers and the health of their industries. For instance, if many of the suppliers are unprofitable and facing financial constraints, continuity of supply could become an issue. If a major customer is facing an uncertain future, you may want to think about how much pain the customer's bankruptcy would cause the company you're analyzing.

Next, you need to be clear about where growth is coming from and where profit is coming from. In the best case, the biggest business, the growth business and the most profitable business will all be the same. Whereas, in the worst case, the biggest business is the unprofitable one that's in decline, the growth business is tiny and unprofitable, and the profitable business is small and not growing.

You could look at Amazon here. Geographically, last year it was the international business that was growing fastest. Does that mean the U.S has reached its peak? Is the U.S saturated? How long do you think it will take for the international business to reach maturity? Will Amazon see diminishing returns as it accesses increasingly smaller and lower-income markets?

I don't have the answers - these are the issues that you need to think about if you're doing fundamental analysis properly!

Industry comparisons

Always compare companies with other companies that have the same business model. Amazon and Walmart may sell similar products to similar customers, but the business models are very different. You can't really compare them. Perhaps in ten years' time, when Amazon has set up more bricks-and-mortar distribution and Walmart has gone further down the e-commerce route, you'll be able to, but I think it's too early right now.

Across companies in a single industry, usually most of the ratios will look similar. Some companies will have higher margins, and you should ask yourself why.

Do they have higher priced products? Do they have lower costs? Or are they more efficiently run? The answer may sometimes be easy to find: other times, you'll have to do a bit of guesswork. Sometimes, it's interesting to track the trends - you can see where one company starts to gain success through cost cutting, for instance.

In the same way, the return on assets is usually fairly similar across an industry because everyone will be using the same kind of assets and paying roughly the same amounts for them. However, you'll find some differences.

For instance, a retailer that uses smaller sites will have different real estate costs from one that concentrates on bigger outlets; and in manufacturing, companies which have invested in making existing facilities smarter may be able to crack out extra profits from having lower setup costs, increased customization and lower waste.

When you come across really pronounced differences, that tells you something important. The same is true with trends - if everyone else is seeing margins squeezed, but one company has margins going up, it's getting something right; if most companies are seeing sales grow fast, but one or two aren't, market share is being won and lost, and you ought to ask why that's happening and look around for explanations.

Sometimes you'll find that one or two of the big players in a sector are private. They may not have a lot in the way of financial figures for you to view, but you can probably find out quite a lot about the size of the business in other ways. You may also be able to find out what their strategy is, particularly if they are owned by a private equity firm that wants to fatten them up for an IPO in a few years.

Watch the ETFs

One interesting way to get a view of the different sectors is to watch sector ETFs. For instance, iShares U.S Regional Banks ETF (IAT) gives you a good feel for how the share prices of small and medium sized U.S regional banks are performing.

Of course, ETFs don't show you the underlying fundamentals of the industry, but they do show you how the broad sector is performing on the stock exchange. Sometimes that's useful to know.

Chapter 6 Quiz

1. When Warren Buffett talks of a 'moat,' what does he mean?
   a. A water filled ditch around a building
   b. That a company has a particular advantage its rivals can't overcome
   c. Market share above 50 percent
   d. A very high return on capital

2. Which of these cost inputs is most significant for an airline?
   a. Raw materials and inventory
   b. Aviation fuel
   c. Marketing costs
   d. Software

3. What is backwards integration?
   a. A fancy way of describing a demerger
   b. Integration that doesn't work
   c. Buying a supplier
   d. Buying an unrelated business

4. High market share can be a mixed blessing. Why?
   a. The market leader is expected to have the lowest prices
   b. The authorities may be interested in anti-trust issues making life difficult for the business
   c. It makes a company an easy target for new entrants
   d. Consumers quickly get bored with the product

5. What do Blackberry, Kodak, Nokia and Blockbuster have in common?
   a. Pictures
   b. Memory chips
   c. Lost out to industry disruption
   d. Low market share

7

Chapter 7: What CEOs say - and what they mean

Analyzing a company's annual report, you may find that there's rather a difference between the breezy optimism of the glossy paper bit, and what you find in the small print financials. Part of that is simply that the two parts of the publication are intended for different audiences. But sometimes, the difference is more of a worry. Fundamental analysis is a great tool for working out whether CEOs mean what they say.

That's one reason I like to read the report back to front. If I've been worried about five or six of the key ratios, and I have some unanswered questions about last year's performance, when I turn to the front and read, "We had a record year, everything in the garden is lovely, and there's apple pie for dessert" (or words to that effect), it makes me worry even more.

On the other hand, if I turn to the front and the CEO fesses up - "We had a few challenges last year, things were tough, here's what we did, it could take 6 months to turn round" - I'm far more likely to think the CEO knows what they are doing.

So, for instance, in the risks facing a company, most of the risks will be ordinary stuff that the lawyers insisted on putting in. It always reminds me of that disclaimer on finance ads that used to tell you, "Warning: stock markets can go up as well as down." (Did I get that right? It certainly felt like that in the 2001 bear market!)

But you might also see a good roundup of what the CEO sees as the risks facing the company. I'm interested in a couple of things in section 1A, the risk statement in the Amazon report.

- "We are impacted by fraudulent or unlawful activities of sellers." Amazon doesn't provide its own products and can't police its sellers. What surprises me here is that this risk comes quite high up in the list - I suspect that means the company's lawyers are not 100% confident about Amazon being able to distance itself from responsibility.
- "We rely on a limited number of shipping companies" - this suggests there is a single weak link in Amazon's chain right here. I would want to keep an eye on what's happening to prices at USPS, DHL and FedEx, for instance.

Is there anything else in there that surprises you?

When you're reading the risk statement, you should also ask yourself if there's anything that you think is a risk, but that isn't included. For instance, I'd be worried if I read an annual report from a bricks-and-mortar retailer and the risk from online competition wasn't included.

Now let's move on and look at how this year is presented. At this point, when I'm researching companies, I like to look at last year's annual report and notes.

- What promises were made?
- What problems were noted?

Then I look at this year's report. Did they deliver on promises?

For instance, if cost cuts were promised, did they happen? Did new products appear on time? How successful were they?

Now obviously, Amazon's 2018 report wasn't going to put "hey guys, we have a pandemic coming in a year and a half" as a problem, but generally, if a business problem appears during the course of a year, it's likely management had an idea it was going to happen earlier. So, I will see if this has been a disappointing year, was there something in last year's report that noted it was going to be challenging.

I also like to test what management is saying against the ratios. If the report says that prices are strong and the market shows high demand, and yet the gross and operating margins declined, I smell a rat (in other words, dishonest behavior).

If the management gives earnings guidance, I want to check out whether they've usually had upside earnings surprises or a few misses. If a company is always missing guidance, it's usually a sign of poor financial controls or poor management - most companies aim to give guidance that they can narrowly beat "managing expectations".

I like to listen to conference calls for companies I'm invested in whenever I can. I could just read the transcript, but you don't get quite the same feedback you do with the audio. For instance:

- Does the CFO sound like they have all the numbers at their fingertips? Can top management answer questions directly without looking things up?

- Does management get rattled? I've heard a CEO getting more and more uneasy the longer the call went on. It sounded like a kid who hadn't done their homework. Sometimes you can hear from their voices that there's a particular subject they're not happy talking about. (That's different from things they *won't* talk about, generally because there's a legal issue involved.)
- Reaction to follow-on questions is particularly telling when the analyst wants more detail or doesn't feel they've got the answer they needed.
- I have, once or twice in my career, heard bullying by management. "That's a stupid question," "I don't even know what you mean by debt maturity", "Are you calling me a liar?". No matter how annoying an analyst is, if management reacts like that, it's problematic. (It's interesting that some analysts recall Enron management acting in this way very shortly before the company's collapse.)

Then on the factual level, compare what the company you're looking at has to say compared with what other companies in the sector are saying. Compare what management is saying with the financial ratios that you're looking at. Do the ratios agree with the statements? Have any questions you had about the numbers been answered in the conference call?

If you can't understand something, and the explanations don't seem convincing, you may be right; the emperor *isn't* wearing any clothes. 'Black boxes' and 'secret algorithms' are fine in the Da Vinci code, but if a CEO is trying to sell you them, and the numbers don't stack up, you're right to walk away.

By the way, while I make time for conference calls, I'd recommend you follow my example and don't bother with annual meetings. You can exercise your vote by proxy. Most of the time, annual meetings are pretty cursory administrative affairs. Only the Berkshire Hathaway meeting is, by all accounts, quite an amazing event, and you now only need to own one $300 B share, rather than one of the $400,000 A shares, to get in.

I would also recommend you keep an eye out for zero content press releases. Some companies want to tell you about their wonderful product, service, or corporate culture every week, and issue large amounts of statements with no facts at all. Managements that do this are very often involved in puffing their own stock, writing PR instead of getting on with running the business properly.

Mind you, if you look at the letter to shareholders in the front of the Amazon report, I find that full of buzzwords and jargon - but you can see that the company is a success. So, make sure you do your due diligence!

'Great management' - a warning

Many people think that assessing the management of a company is a vital part of fundamental analysis. I'm actually going to disagree.

One advantage Wall Street and City analysts have is that they're able to meet management and ask questions directly. They've probably had one-on-one meetings and phone calls a good few times, and they have a chance to size up the CEO's character and that of other executives. A retail investor like ourselves doesn't.

Worse, you're exposed to a lot of media that will tell you that this person is a 'great, hands-on', 'visionary', 'transformative', or whatever, manager. You can just ignore that. People who come across as visionaries may in fact have a far-reaching view of how their industry is going to change over the medium term, or they may just be idiots or even crooks with a few buzzwords and more charisma than they need. What's most important is actually very simple - you need management to be honest. Honest and stupid will do better for shareholders than smart and crooked.

You are best not trying to grade management but assess the way they work. For instance, a particular CEO may always have been able to turn around loss-making companies by cost cutting and by refocusing the product range. I would not necessarily back him if he took over a high growth company. Equally, a CEO who has typically worked in B2B companies (such as accounting software or payroll management) might not do as well in a consumer facing business. Another may be very good at making acquisitions, so you'd expect that if he moves into another company, he'll start doing that quite fast.

If management is visionary and talks a good fight and seems to have good ideas, but the company never makes any money, the CEO is a failure. If the CEO is stodgy, even boring, but produces ever-increasing earnings without going heavily into debt or fiddling the books, we have a success. The numbers tell you how good the management is. And if everyone says the management is brilliant, but the numbers don't bear it out - always, always **believe the numbers**.

Chapter 7 Quiz

1. Why should you read two successive years' annual reports?
    a. For variety
    b. To check management promises against the out-turn in the next year
    c. To check the number of shares hasn't changed
    d. To see whether the branding has changed

2. If the CEO blames poor earnings on high costs, which of these will tell you he's lying?
    a. Head office costs have increased
    b. The operating margin increased
    c. The return on capital declined
    d. Gross margins fell although revenues increased

3. The CEO says the industry is suffering from low demand, but competitors have seen increases in sales. Which of these is *not* an explanation for the apparently contradictory statements?
    a. Competitors are smaller and have increased their market share.
    b. Competitors have lower prices and have attracted business away from the company.
    c. Competitors have 'stuffed' their latest results by recognizing revenue before it should be booked.
    d. The company makes a higher operating profit than its rivals.

4. Why is the risk statement important?
    a. Because it can show you what the CEO thinks are the biggest risks,
    b. Because you have to read it according to investment rules,
    c. Because it contains price-sensitive information,
    d. It isn't.

5. Which of these is not a recommended way of listening to the analyst conference?
    a. Through the Motley Fool website
    b. Through the company's investor relations website
    c. Through dial up, if you're a shareholder and have been invited
    d. By bugging the boardroom

A.Z Penn

8

Chapter 8: What's the price tag?

So far, we just looked around the annual report, and then we practiced calculating different ratios. But now it's time to set a price tag on the company and the shares.

There are quite a few ways that you can do this. In this chapter, I'm going to look at the most usual ones, and then in the next chapter, I'm going to get technical and tell you about a more advanced approach. In fact, there's no single right answer. Any valuation is a matter of judgment as well as number-crunching - an art as well as a science.

First of all, let's look at the P/E ratio. If I told you a business had a P/E ratio of 28, would it be overvalued or undervalued? To know that, you need to know the comparisons.

- First of all, you should know the P/E ratio of the market in general and of larger companies versus smaller companies. But that's not necessarily enough to value a specific company.
- You need to know the *industry comparisons*. What's the average for the sector? That's your first jumping off point.
- You also need to have an idea of the growth rate for the sector. In breweries, for instance, the very mature Anheuser-Busch is valued at 25, which is a much lower P/E ratio than the smaller Boston Beer Co (BBC) at 48. Though BBC had a horrendous 2021, it's expected to grow faster than the big guys in the future. Growth companies within a sector will always be valued at a premium.
- You should also have some idea of the quality of the operations - all the stuff about moats, quality of earnings, whether management keep their promises, whether the brand is good, whether you feel the company is well managed.

However, how much of a premium, or discount, a particular company should be given is very much a matter of judgment.

I find it can sometimes help to set down the P/E ratio (and P/E-to-growth) of each company in a circle. I then compare across competitors in the sector, writing my comments down on the line that links each pair of companies. Comments might include "higher debt risk", "highly concentrated customer base", "unfashionable brands", "losing traction", "reliable dividend payer," "high organic growth", or "too many acquisitions", for instance. I can then keep that page as an easy reference for later on to see if a company is overvalued or undervalued in comparison to its competitors.

That applies to companies which are in a steady state. But sometimes, they're not. For instance, you might have a smaller company that has a one in three chance of getting a major contract which would transform its future prospects. Or you might have a company where analysts are very divided over its growth potential. In that kind of situation, I like to use *expected values* - a statistical method of creating scenarios.

Fundamental Analysis for Beginners

For instance, with the small business and the big contract, I can forecast its earnings with and without the contract, and value the company for either case.

Then, I give the 'with contract' scenario a 33% probability, so I multiply the valuation by 0.33, and since probabilities always add up to 100% (*something* is 100% likely to happen), I multiply the 'without contract' valuation by 0.66.

The correct valuation for the company right now, accounting for both the potential of the new contract and its uncertainty, is the total of those two values.

Let me show you the workings on the next page.

	Without contract	With contract
Earnings	$100m	$300m
P/E ratio	18	18
Value of company	$1,800m	$5,400m
Probability	.66	.33
Value multiplied by probability	$1,188m	$1,782m
Expected value	$1,188m + $1,782m = $2,970m	

I used the same P/E ratio for both cases. In fact, it's possible that if the company got the contract, it might be re-rated (that is, given a higher P/E ratio, but I'm not going to bet on it).

I find expected value really useful to determine what's a fair amount to pay when you have different potential outcomes. It can also be good to look at a range of values.

For instance, you might say that you aren't 100% sure what is the right P/E multiple for a company, but it should probably be valued around the same as other companies in its sector. Rather than just looking at the average, you might consider the range between the highest and lowest P/E ratio in the sector. (Cut out any 'outliers' - for instance, the one company that has an outrageously high multiple because it's rumored to be the subject of a possible takeover bid.)

That would give you a feel for where the share price ought to lie - and how much variation there is between the high, low, and average.

As usual, this will not give you "the answer", but it will help to clarify your thinking.

The conglomerate valuation

You might also look at a company as the sum of the parts. Generally, you wouldn't split the value of a brewery from the value of its plant and property because the brewery couldn't brew beer and distribute it without its brewery and warehouses. But in some cases, either a company possesses assets that it doesn't use in the business, or has a number of different business types, or has assets that could be worth far more if they were used differently.

For instance, a company might operate a small retail business and use its own point-of-sale software. If you value it as a retail business, it might be worth a fairly low multiple of its earnings. But suppose you thought it could sell the software business to a computer firm? You could work out that if the software was sold on a subscription basis to 500 other small retailers at $5,000 a year each, revenues would be $2.5m, and with limited costs, perhaps you could see profits at $2m. Add in expected fast growth, you'd get a multiple of maybe 40 times earnings, which means you could add $80m to your valuation (*if* the sale went ahead).

In the case of a company with different businesses, it's an even simpler job to value the different parts of the business. For example, General Electric has aviation, healthcare, and an energy business. You simply value each area by comparing it with its sector.

This is the way Peter Lynch analyzed General Electric when the stock was trading for almost nothing, and he worked out that the finance business on its own was worth more than the stock market valuation for the entire company.

Looking back to the very beginnings of mobile telecoms, smart investors put money into a rather ordinary electronics company called Racal which had a military radio business. This small business developed into a cellular business and won one of the first two licenses granted to operators in the UK. The rest of Racal, at one point, had a *negative* value once the telecom side had been accounted for.

Sometimes, you'll see a company has a pile of cash. Normally, you'd assume a company has cash that it needs for its day-to-day operations. But if it has a really large amount of cash that it hasn't earmarked for investment, then you might decide to treat that as part of the valuation; work out the cash per share, and add that to the value of the business.

To be quite accurate, you'll need to take interest income out of the earnings statement, though. This is to avoid double counting. If you are taking the cash out of the share price, you should take out interest paid on that cash from the earnings.

Yield, EBITDA, Price/revenue, Price/book

While the P/E ratio is the most commonly used valuation, others are also useful. However, usually, they are secondary to the P/E ratio or used mainly in particular circumstances.

I like to use both yield and price to book as backstops. For instance, if a stock's yield is more than twice the yield on the S&P 500, then if the business is a good one, I think it's unlikely to increase much further. Or if the price to book value falls below 1, then again, I think it's unlikely to fall much further.

However, you need to look out for **dividend traps** and **value traps**.

Sometimes, for instance, a stock has a limited life - a mine that is becoming exhausted, or a technology that is becoming outdated- or it has high debts, a major lawsuit hanging over it (asbestos cases, for instance, lots of employees of companies like Manville Corporation had asbestosis as a result of their work. Manville Corporation actually declared bankruptcy as the claims against it were so large it couldn't pay them.) or some other major liability that could damage the business beyond recovery.

Or, in the case of dividend traps, the company doesn't have enough earnings to cover the dividend, or for other reasons, the dividend is about to be cut. You need to be quite careful - and however careful you are, sometimes you'll make the wrong call. That's inevitable.

EBITDA and revenue multiples are useful when you are looking at companies that don't currently make a profit. Although some investors are suspicious of these ratios, there's nothing wrong with them; you just need to be careful that you have a good understanding of how the company will get from loss making to money making and that the business model works.

The problem with the tech bubble wasn't so much that the wrong bases of valuation were being used, it was because some of the companies didn't have good business models and never ended up making a profit at all.

EBITDA multiples can also be useful for looking at companies in a sector where companies' financial positions and depreciation or amortization requirements are very different. If one company has a lot of debt and another has cash, when you look at EBIT or EBITDA you're comparing profitability at a level before interest, so their financial situations don't affect the comparison. You get a feel for the underlying business.

If one company has made a big acquisition and has large amortization expenses, and the other doesn't, again, the comparison at EBITDA level lets you see underlying performance without the difference that comes from the fact that one company bought a business and the other built it organically.

And of course, EBITDA is also useful for companies that are young and producing cash flow but not profits.

Price to revenues is also useful. I often use it when I'm looking at companies with below standard profitability to see what they would be worth if management got to grips with the operations. But I would never use it as my main valuation multiple because we're interested in revenues mainly as one of the factors that drives profits.

So really a company should be valued on profits, and revenues are only separately useful if there's some reason that a profit valuation won't work properly - like the company is in a *turnaround* situation.

Instead, I might work out what profits *should* be once the cost issues are addressed and then look at the P/E multiple on that scenario.

Analysts tend to restrict themselves to forecasts - actually, sometimes a back-of-envelope working for a 'what if?' scenario is more useful. What if gross margins were brought up to average for the sector? What if head office costs were trimmed by 10%? what if...

I promise this is the last time I'm going to talk about GameStop.

Let's put a few of these valuation methods together and have a look at GameStop. It's actually an interesting exercise because all your bargain-hunting instincts will say, "Hey, look, this share dropped from $300 to $90, it has to be cheap!".

So, let's put that to the test.

In the table below, I show GameStop's basic valuation criteria as they stood when the short squeeze was going on;

P/E ratio	617
Price/sales	1.4

GameStop can be compared in two different directions.

First of all, it's in video games, so you could compare it to video game developers like Take-Two (TTWO), Electronic Arts (EA), or Activision Blizzard (ATVI).

They are highly valued, with trailing price/earnings ratios from 23 to 57 times and a price to sales of an average of 6.18 times. That is, (7.25 + 5.6 + 5.7) / 3.

The table below shows the trailing 12 month P/E ratio and price/sales for ATVI, TTWO and EA.

	ATVI	TTWO	EA
Trailing 12 month P/E ratio	23.7	34	57
Price/sales	7.25	5.6	5.7

However, there are a couple of big differences between these businesses and GameStop. First of all, they own the content that they sell. Secondly, their financials are in much better shape than GameStop's (these 3 developers are profitable and growing their sales).

So perhaps they should be valued more highly than GameStop.

In fact, the opposite was the case in terms of the P/E ratio. GameStop was valued at 617 times earnings...

But, that's not the case anymore. Now, GameStop is back in losses, so the P/E ratio is irrelevant. And the shares are drifting.

The other companies to which you could compare GameStop are the big retailers. Who competes with it in selling video games and much more? Why not look at Walmart, Best Buy, and Amazon.

The table below shows the trailing 12 month P/E ratio and price/sales for Walmart, Best Buy and Amazon.

	Walmart	Best Buy	Amazon
Trailing 12 month P/E ratio	28	9.3	47.46
Price/sales	0.67	0.47	3.37

When you look at the Walmart and Best Buy, then GameStop is worth way, way less than you'd think. And Walmart is huge; it has a dominant market position.

It's only if you take Amazon as a comparison that you'd think GameStop is cheap as Amazon has a higher price/sales.

But again, Amazon is a dominant market player, and it has a huge growth rate, and it's on the right side of the bricks/chips retail divide (bricks = high street or shopping centre, chips = e-commerce).

I may be wrong. GameStop is apparently managing to get its sales back to growth and is on the brink of breaking even. It might justify its share price. But my feeling when I look at these valuations is that it has a long way to go.

GameStop's top team are smart, that I will admit! I'm just impressed that a company whose market valuation in 2000 was just $400m managed to utilize the WallStreetBets short squeeze to launch a $1.5 *billion* share issue.

Subtractions from value

There are a few items that need to be subtracted from the value of a company when you make a valuation. These can all be found in the notes on the annual report, and the main ones are:

- off-balance-sheet debt
- off-balance-sheet liabilities such as pension schemes
- potential losses from litigation.

Taking off the liabilities - all the things that you know the company will have to pay, or may have to pay, and are quantifiable. You're taking off the worst case.

Often, off balance sheet debt is something that the company will end up having to pay one way or another. You would subtract them only if you think they are chickens that will actually come home to roost.

For instance, in the case of a company with a huge lawsuit brought by former employees for terminal illness caused by unhealthy work conditions, I might take the view that the company is likely to lose or to have to settle at a high price. I'd then subtract that amount from the P/E ratio-based valuation of the business to arrive at the *intrinsic value*.

Chapter 8 Quiz

1. What is a dividend trap?
    a. A kind of piggy bank for investors
    b. A company that has a high yield but is financially risky
    c. Like a honey trap, a way to catch spies
    d. When a company doesn't pay dividends at all

2. An expected value is based on the valuation under different scenarios weighted according to their;
    a. Severity
    b. Profitability
    c. Probability
    d. Alphabetical order

3. Which is the 'gold standard' valuation ratio?
    a. Price to book
    b. Return on assets
    c. Price to revenues
    d. The price/earnings ratio

4. When might you want to use price/revenues or price/EBITDA?
    a. When the company isn't making a profit
    b. When the company has high debt
    c. When the other analysts use it
    d. When the price to book is below 1

5. Which of these would not affect your assessment of the right P/E ratio for a company?
    a. Several negative earnings surprises in the last two years
    b. High market share
    c. The company's growth prospects
    d. The rate of inflation

9

Chapter 9: 50 cents now or 10 bucks later?

Fundamental analysis looks for the 'intrinsic value' of a stock. However, so far, I've only talked about how to compare one stock with others. That gives you a comparative valuation, but not an absolute one. In other words, we might know that Amazon trades on a higher valuation than Microsoft or a lower valuation than Tesla, but we still don't know whether that's right. We can't set a price in dollars.

The **discounted cash flow (DCF)** model can give you an absolute answer as to how much a company is worth - if you get your assumptions right. It's a bit complex, both as a concept and in the calculation, so this may be the **toughest chapter** yet - but it's a crucial one so perhaps read it over a couple of times to fully grasp everything.

I want you to read it with a spreadsheet open if you can, and to play around with the spreadsheet, trying different discount factors, different rates of growth, and different scenarios, till you feel quite at home with the process.

To understand how the DCF model works, you need to understand that money exists in the length of time, and that its value depends on duration on the time that you have to wait till you receive it.

If I borrowed a certain sum of money and said I'd pay it back tomorrow, next month, next year, or in 10 years' time, your response might be very different depending on the length of time I wanted to borrow it. People say, "time is money", and money actually has what is called a *time value*. You could represent that by the interest rate on a loan, for instance.

Let's take that up a notch and think about it in terms of actual numbers rather than just emotionally. If I have $100 right now, it will be worth more in a year's time because I will have had *interest* paid on it. So, for instance, at 10% interest (just to make the math a bit easier), it's worth:

- $110 after a year ($100 x 10%)
- $121 after two years ($110 x 10%)
- $133 after three years ($121 x 10%)
- $146 after four years, and ($133 x 10%)
- $161 after five years. ($146 x 10%)

Got it?

Now, look at that backwards. If I promise to pay you $161 in five years' time, what is that promise worth right now?

Assuming my credit is good, it's worth $100.

Or if I promise to pay you $110 in one year, it's worth $100 now.

That, in essence, is how compound interest builds up forward (the compounding effect), and how you **discount back** a future payment.

So now let's look at a company, and we can see that it will deliver cash flow every year. It's a bit more difficult to analyze because it's not just a single payment that you have to discount back; so, you'd need to discount next year's dividend back 12 months, but the year after that, you'd need to discount back by two years, and the year after that by three years, and so on. So, there's a bit of added complexity, but the idea is the same.

In fact, I've got a couple of ways I could define the company's return to the investor.

- I could value the flow of dividends. *Theoretically*, the value of a stock is the value of all future dividend payments. But there are enough stocks that don't pay a dividend to make this less useful than it might be. It also ignores potential returns through capital growth, which make up at least a third of equity returns.
- I could value future net cash flow - the cash generated after investment has been taken care of. This is what I'd do if I was planning to acquire 100% of the company, and it's the way most analysts value companies traded on the stock market.

By the way, the math in this chapter is a bit complex when you have to express it in terms of formulas. However, most spreadsheets have a function to help you work out discounted values, so don't let that bother you. In Microsoft Excel, it's called XNPV in the 'Financial' function category and in LibreOffice you have the NPV function. There are several tutorials online that you can watch to learn how to use these functions.

Constant dividend model

Okay, I'm going to look at the **constant dividend model** first (it's also called the Gordon Growth Model). Even though it's of limited value, it's actually quite interesting because if you use this, you could start out with a bond and a stock that pays the same yield right now, and see the difference over 10 years in the returns you get.

When I started writing this chapter, I could have bought 10-year U.S Treasuries yielding at **1.94%** according to GuruFocus Yield Curve (which is a reliable source).

(By the way, you may have noticed I used 1.92% to calculate WACC in an earlier chapter which I had wrote a few days earlier. Of course, the yield changes as bond prices go up and down daily, which is why you might like to revisit your calculations from time to time, as the 10-year U.S Treasuries can change every day!)

Therefore, if I put in $10,000 in U.S Treasuries today, I would get $194 a year in yield, every year for 10 years. (That is, $10,000 x 1.94% = $194.)

Just for the sake of the example so you can see where the excess gains on equities come from, I found a stock from a stock screener on Morningstar to find dividend yields between 0 and 2%, then ranked stocks highest to lowest by yield so I could find the closest to 1.94%, which led me to come across Advance Auto Parts (AAP) stock which has a 1.94% yield.

Now let's say I put in $10,000 in AAP. This will get me $194 this year in yield. But looking at the last five years, earnings grew by 9% a year on average, according to Yahoo Finance. (You can find it under the "Financial" tab)

Therefore, I'm going to moderate my expectations and forecast earnings growing by only **4%** in the future. That's because even though the companies have had a 9% on average in the previous five years, and are expecting 10% growth in earnings in 2022 (according to an article by The Motley Fool), at some rate, eventually, growth will slow down over the longer term. And the model we use for calculating earnings is a very *long-term model* - in fact, it assumes growth in perpetuity, which is a much longer investment time horizon, hence *4%* would be a moderate expectation for us to be on the safe side.

So that would mean for AAP, you'd get $202 earnings in year two ($194 x 1.04 = $202), and $210 earnings in year three ($202 x 1.04 = $210), and so on.

There's a formula that will let us take a shortcut to find out the value. It's called the *constant dividend model*, and the formula is:

Value = Next year's dividend / (discount rate - dividend growth rate)

So, for U.S Treasuries, next year's coupon is $194, and there is no growth.

We can take the discount rate of 1.94%, as U.S Treasuries are usually considered risk-free since the U.S government isn't going to default on its bonds. And 10-year Treasuries are an appropriately long term investment to compare to equities. And there's no dividend growth rate.

So, if we plot in the formula, we get *$194 / 1.94% = $10,000*, which is, of course, what we invested. Hence there's no growth.

But for the company AAP, two things change. First of all, there's a *growth rate of 4%* (which we moderately forecasted). And secondly, because companies represent a higher risk than investing in the U.S Government Treasury Bonds, therefore, the discount rate is higher for companies.

I'm not going to go through how you calculate it, but right now, most analysts are using an equity discount rate of around **6%**. I tracked this down in various analyst pieces. It reflects over a decade of low/negative interest rates.

(It's worth noting that different analysts use different rates, very rarely do they all agree; and that using DCF properly is about understanding the way it works and being able to plug in different data or different rates to test your hypotheses, rather than expecting a "computer says yes" answer. Also, this is not chapter and verse, and it won't give you 'right' answers. But it will give you an idea of what long term value might be and what it's made up of. And you can then examine what a slowdown in the growth rate would do to your valuation, or what the need for a big chunk of capital spending would do to it.)

So, I can calculate next year's dividend of $202 and then divide it by the *discount rate of 6%*, less the *dividend growth rate of 4%* (which we had moderately forecasted).

So, *$202 / (6% - 4%)*, or simplified *($202 / 2%) = $10,100,* which is a very small amount more than we paid for the stock.

That additional *$100* from the $10,000 initial investment is the current value of that dividend growth, compared with the bonds in U.S Treasuries which have an unchanging coupon.

You may already have spotted a problem with this model, though.

You'd get a negative value if the dividend growth is higher than the discount rate (for example, if we had *4% - 6% = -2%*). And right now, many companies have dividend growth higher than the discount rate, which basically means you can't do the calculation for the constant dividend model in this that case.

So, let's move on to the second and more useful method, fully *discounted cash flow.*

Discounted cash flow

For this method, you'll need to build a spreadsheet and plug in numbers from the annual report. Remember that Wall Street analysts need to show *absolutely* everything, but we don't have to impress anyone, so we can cut a few corners in simplifying the process.

Before we start, I would definitely suggest you download my free bonus #3 on Amazon's DCF Model Revealed. It would be essential for you to understand the calculations and formulas I discuss in this section live on your computer. Please visit: www.az-penn.com *to download the spreadsheet for free.*

The first part of the table looks like this. We have the five years at the top, and the different headings on the left. I have not plotted in the figures yet, but this is the basic template to get us started.

	Years (in $m)				
	1	2	3	4	5
Net Income					
Depreciation					
Working Capital					
Other non-cash items					
	$0.00	$0.00	$0.00	$0.00	$0.00
Capital Expenditure					
Disposals					
	$0.00	$0.00	$0.00	$0.00	$0.00
Cash Flow	$0.00	$0.00	$0.00	$0.00	$0.00

So, now let's fill it in for Amazon (I'd recommend you turn on your computer and do the following steps with me).

First of all, I'm going to Zacks (zacks.com) to look for AMZN, then under 'More Research' on the left-hand side, I'll look at the 'Full Company Report'.

In the 'Company Summary' section, I can see an estimated long term EPS growth rate of 28.4% (at the time of writing this, though the rate may differ when you're looking at it).

But, wow, isn't that high!?

I'm going to assume that probably, EBIT will grow at about the same rate. So, taking last year's report as the basis, I can calculate the growth rate for all the various heading from the table above.

Net income last year was $21,331m, so I'm going to multiply that by the growth rate of 1.28 (that is, 100% + 28% growth), and that's my first year's net income here.

So that's, $21,331m x 1.28 = *$27,304m* for year 1 net income.

For year 2, it's going to be year 1 figure of $27,304m x 1.28 = *$34,949m.*

Then I need a formula for year 3, 4 and 5 that multiplies the previous year's net income by 1.28 growth rate, and I can fill the whole line in for all five years for net income.

Now the spreadsheet looks like this for net income:

	Years (in $m)				
	1	2	3	4	5
Net Income	$27,304	$34,949	$44,734	$57,260	$73,293
Depreciation					
Working Capital					
Other non-cash items					
	$27,304	$34,949	$44,734	$57,260	$73,293
Capital Expenditure					
Disposals					
	$0	$0	$0	$0	$0
Cash Flow	$27,304	$34,949	$44,734	$57,260	$73,293

I'll admit, this is very basic. If you were doing this for real, you'd check out analysts' forecasts on Yahoo Finance to see if yours were similar or different, and think about why yours are different (if they are). It's fascinating - there's a huge difference between the low and high forecasts, with the low forecast for 2022 EPS at $25.78 and the high forecast at $75.44!

For me, forecasting is about thinking through all the fundamentals, forecasting revenues, forecasting margins, or if I know particular costs (like aviation fuel for instance) forecasting those. But for those without the modelling, using analyst estimates is a perfectly good short cut.

And you'd want to read through the annual report to see if there are any impacts from an increase in the number of shares issued (though, in this case, there aren't) or any expected chunky capital spending. If you have share issues, then you may end up diluted (that is, getting a smaller share of future earnings than you'd expected).

If there is big capital spending, there might be negative cash flow for a year or two, or the company might need to raise money, which would result in dilution.

Amazon is a company in a relatively steady state. It gets trickier when you have a company that's making a big change to its business - whether it's just de-merged a non-core business, made a big acquisition, or has a huge investment or a massive new product launch. You can build all of those into this DCF model - you just have to think through what you know.

But for now, I'm going to cheat by multiplying them by the 28% EPS growth rate. I'm going to just fill in all the other figures in the same basic way, starting from the 2020 annual report.

And now in the example below, I have five whole years of cash flow.

	Years (in $m)				
	1	**2**	**3**	**4**	**5**
Net Income	$27,304	$34,949	$44,734	$57,260	$73,293
Depreciation	$32,321	$41,371	$52,955	$67,782	$86,761
Working Capital	$17,256	$22,088	$28,272	$36,188	$46,321
Other non-cash items	$11,786	$15,086	$19,310	$24,717	$31,638
	$88,667	$113,493	$145,271	$185,948	$238,013
Capital Expenditure	-$76,302	-$97,667	-$125,013	-$160,017	-$204,822
Disposals	$0	$0	$0	$0	$0
	-$76,302	-$97,667	-$125,013	-$160,017	-$204,822
Cash Flow	$12,365	$15,827	$20,258	$25,931	$33,191

Now let's talk about discounting back. The easy way to do this is you can show the net present value (NPV) of each year's income. First of all, you need to work out the discount factor for each year.

The formula is this:

1 / (1 + discount rate) to the power of the period number.

The discount rate of 6% is expressed as 0.06.

So, *1 + 0.06 = 1.06.*

Then computing in the formula for the first year, it's simply: *1 / (1 + 0.06) = 0.94* for the discount factor.

For the second year, you need 1.06 to the power of 2. Or, you can do 1.06 squared, which you can calculate easily as 1.06 x 1.06.

But if you carry on doing that every year, it's long-winded, it takes forever, so use the POWER function in the spreadsheet instead: you get a formula =POWER(1.06,2) for year 2, =POWER(1.06,3) for year 3, =POWER(1.06,4) for year 4, and finally =POWER(1.06,5) for year 5.

Example below shows you how the =POWER formula should be computed in Microsoft Excel for year 2.

fx	=POWER(1.06,2)

C	D	E	F
	1.124		

The table below shows all 5 years after using the =POWER formula in Excel.

1	1.06
2	1.124
3	1.191
4	1.262
5	1.338

Once you've done that for all five years, all you need is to calculate one divided by each result, and you have the discount rates for all the years.

*Year 1 = 1 / 1.06 = **0.94***

*Year 2 = 1 / 1.124 = **0.89***

*Year 3 = 1 / 1.191 = **0.84***

*Year 4 = 1 / 1.262 = **0.79***

*Year 5 = 1 / 1.338 = **0.75***

The table below shows you the final computed figures of the formulas above.

Years	Discount Rates
1	0.94
2	0.89
3	0.84
4	0.79
5	0.75

Yes, that was geeky stuff. Don't worry, once you've built a spreadsheet with your discount rates in, you'll be able to copy it again and again and again.

Next, simply take the cash flow figure and multiply it by the discount rate to get the NPV of cash flows for each year.

So, year 1 = $12,365m x 0.94 = **$11,623m**

Year 2 = $15,826m x 0.89 = **$14,086m**

Year 3 = $20,259m x 0.84 = **$17,017m**

Year 4 = $25,932m x 0.79 = **$20,485m**

Year 5 = $33,191m x 0.75 = **$24,893m**

And finally, add the NPV figures together to arrive at the total value of five years of Amazon earnings of **$88,104m.**

The table below includes the discount factors for the five years, NPV of cash flows for the five years and the total NPV of cash flows computed.

	Years (in $m)				
	1	2	3	4	5
Net Income	$27,304	$34,949	$44,734	$57,260	$73,293
Depreciation	$32,321	$41,371	$52,955	$67,782	$86,761
Working Capital	$17,256	$22,088	$28,272	$36,188	$46,321
Other non-cash items	$11,786	$15,086	$19,310	$24,717	$31,638
	$88,667	$113,493	$145,271	$185,948	$238,013
Capital Expenditure	-$76,302	-$97,667	-$125,013	-$160,017	-$204,822
Disposals	$0	$0	$0	$0	$0
	-$76,302	-$97,667	-$125,013	-$160,017	-$204,822
Cash Flow	$12,365	$15,827	$20,258	$25,931	$33,191
Discount Factors	0.94	0.89	0.84	0.79	0.75
NPV of Cash Flows	$11,623	$14,086	$17,017	$20,485	$24,893
Total NPV of Cash Flows	$88,104				

As a quick check, the NPV of cash flow number you get should always be *less* than the cash flow figure because you've had to wait for the money (the present value of a future sum is always less than the future value, reflecting the time value of money - the fact that you have to wait for it.) **This is the NPV of the cash flow for that year.**

Now I have a problem. The problem is that I've only calculated what Amazon is worth if it keeps going for five years and then liquidates at nil value.

When you use DCF calculations within a business, it's often for limited-time investments, like a mine that would eventually be exhausted or a power plant with a useful life of 20 years. So, they reach the end of the period, and the plant is decommissioned.

But with Amazon, you'd expect it to keep going, maybe at a lower rate of growth. So, there are two ways that you can build that into the calculation.

- You can think about what Amazon shares will be worth on a P/E ratio basis in five years' time and then discount that back.
- Or you can assume that Amazon will grow in perpetuity by a certain amount and work out a terminal value with a formula similar to the previous one we used in the *constant dividend model*.

A terminal value is what we expect the company to be worth in x years' time when we end the DCF calculation. So basically, we're saying we will get this cash flow which we forecasted for x years, and after year 2022 + x years, we will sell the company for what it's worth at the time.

Looking forward five years, I think Amazon will still be a growth stock. Maybe, not growing quite as fast. It will probably still be dominant in e-commerce, though Walmart might be doing some catching up.

So, it will probably still trade at a premium to the market. I don't know where the market will be trading, so let's take a long term average P/E ratio for S&P 500 over the last 30-40 years. That gives us a 16 times P/E ratio, according to MacroTrends.

I would assume Amazon will get 50% more because it's fast growing and has a dominant market position with high returns. So that'll give us a P/E ratio of 24, and a terminal value of **$1,759,032m** (that is, the last cash flow forecast in year 5 of $73,293 x 24 P/E ratio).

Then, *adding* the terminal value to the NPV of years 1 to 5, which is $88,104m. And this gives us a total of **$1,847,136m** (or $1.847trn), which compares with the $1.5trn market capitalization today (in March 2022).

The market capitalization is one of the numbers you see anywhere on the internet that you look up stock prices - it's an absolutely basic number. Of course, you can always check it against shares in issue in the annual report if you are suspicious.

If the terminal value is higher than market capitalization, that might mean the stock is a bargain. Or it might mean our valuation is too optimistic.

So, can we assume that Amazon is trading at a bargain right now? Well, yes. But do I really believe that? No. I think the terminal value accounts for far too high a percentage of the total valuation.

I think what I'd rather do - and this might be worth doing - is actually run a 20-year full model and get the discounted value from that model instead of just doing five years. And I'd be making some assumptions about much reduced growth during the second decade. You cannot always be right. In fact, Amazon might not even look like the same business in 20 years' time, it might be a drone delivery company. But you're trying to assess the shares with the best assumptions that you can.

So, let's try the other way. How fast do I think Amazon can continue growing? A 10% growth rate would be fairly modest in the medium term, and I don't see any reason the company couldn't get that through geographical expansion and increased market penetration.

But in fact, we're looking at *perpetuity* here. We're looking maybe 20, 30, 40 years ahead. So over that period, will Amazon still be growing faster than the economy or should we assume it grows at the same level as GDP of 3% (according to major economics websites).

I think for the early part of the period, it will be growing faster than the GDP rate.

Anyway, do you remember WACC? It's the weighted average cost of the company's finance, split between equity and debt. I'm not going to go through all the calculations, but for Amazon, it's 8% (which I found through a number of quant websites and analyst reports, and that's pretty much what I'd expect for a major corporation).

The formula below is terminal value based on **cash flow (CF) in perpetuity**, rather than terminal P/E ratio which I calculated previously.

Year 5 cash flow x (1 + perpetual growth rate) / WACC - perpetual growth rate.

So, I can plug in the numbers into the formula as;

$33,191m x (1 + 3%) / (8% - 3%) or simply, $34,186m / 5% = **$683,735m.**

Then, *adding* the terminal value to the NPV of years 1 to 5, which is $88,105m. And this gives us a total of **$771,839m.**

A bit different from the other figure, and even when you add in the NPV of the first five years' cash flows, it's a lot lower than the company's current market capitalization.

The table below shows the complete cash flows, and terminal value-based estimations for Amazon for the next 5 years.

	Years (in $m)				
	1	2	3	4	5
Net Income	$27,304	$34,949	$44,734	$57,260	$73,293
Depreciation	$32,321	$41,371	$52,955	$67,782	$86,761
Working Capital	$17,256	$22,088	$28,272	$36,188	$46,321
Other non-cash items	$11,786	$15,086	$19,310	$24,717	$31,638
	$88,667	$113,493	$145,271	$185,948	$238,013
Capital Expenditure	-$76,302	-$97,667	-$125,013	-$160,017	-$204,822
Disposals	$0	$0	$0	$0	$0
	-$76,302	-$97,667	-$125,013	-$160,017	-$204,822
Cash Flow	$12,365	$15,827	$20,258	$25,931	$33,191
Discount Factors	0.94	0.89	0.84	0.79	0.75
NPV of Cash Flows	$11,623	$14,086	$17,017	$20,485	$24,893
Total NPV of Cash Flows	$88,104				
Terminal Value Based on P/E Ratio					$1,759,032
Total Value					$1,847,136
Terminal Value Based on CF in Perpetuity					$683,735
Total Value					$771,839

I was worried enough by the way my DCF analysis undervalued Amazon's current valuation so I looked Amazon DCF valuations on the internet. Alphaspread has an automatic valuation system that suggests Amazon is 31% overvalued. A couple of other commentators had similar views. However, Wall Street has Amazon down as a 'buy' with a target price 43% higher than the current share price - so according to them, it's undervalued.

Pros and cons of DCF

What I'd like you to do as an exercise is to build your own spreadsheet and then play around with it.

For instance, what happens if you assume a 4% perpetual growth rate? What happens if you think earnings growth will run at 50% in year one, then 40% in year two, then 28% year three? It could be fun to jot your different estimates of Amazon's value on a piece of paper.

And now, think about it the other way round. What do you have to do to the assumptions to justify today's market capitalization? Are you happy with those assumptions?

I hope you'll have seen by trying those ideas out that a small change in one of the assumptions can lead to a much greater change in the DCF valuation. This is one of the key disadvantages of this method - in particular, the discount rate you use, and the growth rate you use, will 'swing' the valuation one way or another.

So, it's important that you don't use the DCF as some kind of scientific method which will 'tell' you what the value is - it's better used, at least in my opinion, as a way of exploring which assumptions need to be correct to justify a given value.

For instance, you might like to use DCF analysis together with a number of scenarios to create an expected value. Or you might want to use it simply as a way of examining what underlying assumptions analysts are making when they come up with a target price.

Let's look at some of the other **disadvantages** of the DCF valuation.

- One thing I really dislike is that the terminal value often accounts for most of the valuation. If you're using a five year ahead P/E ratio as your valuation, I wouldn't think that it gives you better information than you'd get by using today's P/E ratio. And at least you can guess that this year's earnings forecasts are probably pretty close to the actual result, whereas the further out you go, the less probable it is your forecasts will be accurate.
- The model's dependence on forecast growth rates makes it particularly unsuitable for valuing the very companies where it's used the most, early-stage technology companies and start-ups.
- The model tends to use smooth growth predictions. That makes it most suitable for businesses with smooth and predictable cash flows, such as utilities, or companies with subscription or rental business models.

On the other hand, the DCF does have the advantage of producing an absolute value using a set of clear assumptions. As long as you remember the IT saying, "Garbage in, garbage out", you'll get a lot of mileage out of the DCF model without being deceived into believing it as a flawless method.

By the way, "Garbage in, garbage out" means that what you get out of a computer is only as good as the data you input. Put in faulty data and you'll get a useless answer.

Other **advantages** of using a DCF model are:

- it can help value a company that may have a couple of years of below-average earnings as you are looking at the value of earnings over a period rather than at earnings at one particular point,
- it's about cash flow, not earnings;
- and it includes medium term growth rather than just looking at the next two years.

Choosing a discount rate

There are numerous different ways to choose a discount rate. Quite often, the company's WACC is used. That may be sensible, as it relates the company's value to the amount it has to pay to fund its operations, but it means your valuation of one company may be based on a discount rate very different from your valuation of another.

You can use the 10-year Treasury rate or a corporate bond yield which you can find using FINRA's TRACE database. But the 10-year Treasury rate is a risk-free rate; the U.S government is extremely unlikely to default. On the other hand, investing in equities are riskier, so investors get a *risk premium* (that is, investors want to be paid more for the higher risk of holding them).

That's why most analysts use a blended rate (because it assesses the company's returns in terms of what it actually costs the company to fund its operations), by adding the *risk-free rate* (the rate on 10-year Treasuries) to the excess *return of the market* over *risk free returns*, multiplied by the *beta* of the stock, which you can find on most finance websites.

RFR + [(market return / RFR) x Beta].

Frankly, I don't think you need to do that. Use a standard rate representing equity market returns over the long term. If you use something like 8% you won't go too far wrong. If you use 8% then you're basing your assessment on long term actual outturns for all equities.

This has two advantages. First, you don't have to do all those calculations every time you do a DCF valuation. And secondly, you know that all your valuations use the same basis.

Forecasting

This is another thing you might not find in many books about fundamental analysis, as they tend to concentrate on analyzing historical figures. But I think it's worth having a go at making your own forecasts.

It's a great way to find out how the business works, particularly if you've built in industry-specific data like occupancy rates in a hotel business. It also makes you examine your thoughts about the future; is it consistent to think a hotel business can keep growing without spending any money opening new hotels, for instance? By attempting to forecast the cash flow, you'll find out whether your revenue expectations are incompatible with your ideas of capital spending.

Be clear about the two or three main factors that affect the business. For instance, for a retailer, things like volumes, mark-up (which gives you your gross margin), and property costs are the big three.

With a consultancy firm, hours worked and billed, and the hourly rate are the big drivers, so you'll want to work out some ratios based on employee numbers and salary costs.

With retail banks, the two big factors are interest (the interest rate they have to pay on deposits, the interest rate they get from lending money out, and the difference between the two), and the cost of running the branch network.

A good exercise for you to do right now would be to pick three or four different stocks and think about what are the key drivers for their business. If you have friends who are interested in investment this can make quite an enjoyable discussion over a few cups of coffee. (By the way, coffee is *not* one of Starbucks' 'big three' - coffee beans have historically accounted for less than 10% of Starbucks' costs. Interesting?)

Fundamental Analysis for Beginners

It's easy to build a massively complex spreadsheet. I made one for an airline once that linked its profits to jet fuel prices, passenger numbers, the average lease cost of a Boeing 737, employee numbers, currencies, the mix of long haul versus short haul business, and a half dozen other factors. I was really proud of it until it went live. I had managed to forecast British Airways losing more than its market capitalization, and most analysts thought it was going to make a profit.

For once, the other analysts were right, and I was wrong.

The trouble with that spreadsheet was that I couldn't see the wood for the trees. That's why you should concentrate on just the most important factors - and that's why you probably shouldn't use the company's formal income statement as your basis for the spreadsheet. Simplify as much as you can. No one's ever going to ask you to explain your workings; the important thing is that you understand them yourself.

When you've done your forecast, take a look at the analyst consensus. Compare your own ideas with the analysts'. If you're wildly adrift, don't assume you've got it wrong - ask yourself what the differences in assumptions are. You might be right. Or you might have missed something - like the effect of currency movements on foreign earnings, or a lawsuit you didn't know about.

Analyst consensus is available on most finance websites like Yahoo Finance or Zacks. You'll usually see the average and the range of forecasts plus buy or sell recommendations, and the number of analysts. Obviously if there are 23 analysts predicting around 25 cents for Big Stock with a range of 24.5 cents earnings to 25.55 cents, that's very different from having just two analysts looking at Itsy Bitsy Corporation with predictions of 20 cents and 59 cents!

Also, important to check, where given, the dates of recommendations and forecasts, as sometimes a year-old forecast gets left up when an analyst hasn't bothered to update for whatever reason.

It's sometimes interesting to see how widespread the analysts are. Sometimes, they are all clustered around the same area pretty tightly. Other times, there's just a single outlier, and sometimes the forecasts are all over the place. If they can't even agree amongst themselves, your guess is as good as theirs. Alternatively, if all of them agree, and you think differently, if you're right, you've probably found a great profit-making opportunity.

Chapter 9 Quiz

1. Which of these is not a major cost for a hotel chain?
   a. Staff
   b. Property costs
   c. Raw materials
   d. Marketing and finance costs

2. Which of these is a major weakness of DCF valuations?
   a. They are not easy to calculate
   b. Changing the inputs even slightly can change the valuation a lot
   c. They don't use the same accounting treatment as the income statement
   d. No one ever talks about them on CNN

3. Discounting to get a net present value is the reverse of
   a. The compounding effect
   b. The Coriolis effect
   c. The carryover effect
   d. The catch-up effect

4. What kind of company is most suitable for DCF analysis?
   a. One with predictable cash flows
   b. One that isn't making a profit
   c. One that has a lot of debt
   d. One that begins with I

5. Which of these is crucial to building an earnings forecast?
   a. Inside information
   b. An advanced econometrics software package
   c. A good forecast for economic growth
   d. The two or three key drivers of costs

A.Z Penn

10

Chapter 10: Macro vs Micro, or Top Down vs Bottom Up

Stocks don't exist in a void, nor do the companies in which you own shares. They exist in the real world, in the larger economy, and they are subject to big economic trends and to socio-demographic trends, like the growth in single-person households and the increased proportion of older people in the population.

When you do fundamental analysis looking at individual companies, you're doing 'bottom up' analysis - starting with the details of the company itself. That lends itself to a stock-picking approach, trying to find excellent businesses to invest in at the right price.

But you can also carry out 'top down' analysis. That means looking at socio-economic trends and then focusing on the stocks that are likely to do well in that situation. For instance, with an increasingly aging population, you might decide you want to look at healthcare, pharmaceuticals, and medical and elder care REITs.

Or you might decide to look at stocks involved in renewable energy, sustainable materials to replace plastics, and other environmentally sustainable niches.

Let me say that some people will find they make really good calls here, others not. Top down can be useful, but it's a matter of style. I personally love reading *Wired* for stuff that takes modern tech almost as far as science fiction, which I find quite challenging - but that doesn't do my investing any good at all. It's just fun.

I find bottom-up analysis gives me a much better bang for my buck. Your mileage, as they say, might differ.

The same goes for fund managers. Some, like George Soros and Stanley Druckenmiller, make big top-down bets and they've made them very successfully. Others, like Warren Buffett, are very much bottom-up guys. Some sit nearer the middle - Peter Lynch is best known for his bottom-up bets, but he knew how to use economic data to spot interesting situations in cyclical stocks.

Where to find economic data

You can obviously find economic data in the media - economic stats are always well covered on TV and in the press. But to do proper analysis, you need more than the latest number. You need a full run of the relevant stats.

Look on the U.S Department of Commerce site and you can find full runs of economic, environmental and demographic data. You'll also find the release schedule for economic indicators. You should also cast an eye over the Conference Board (www.conference-board.org), where you can find global economic indicators, including other areas of the world as well as the U.S. So, for instance, if you had invested in a couple of stocks with important operations in the Far East, you can access data from Japan, China and South Korea. However, a lot of the content has to be paid for.

Particular data series to look at are:

- GDP - Gross Domestic Product. This is the total size of the economy as a whole. It's the growth (or decline) in the overall number, that is the important factor here.
- The Conference Board produces a 'Leading Economic Index' (LEI), which uses various indicators to find the peaks and troughs in the business cycle.
- Inflation has not been an important factor for most of the past 30 years, but this could change as wage rises and soaring oil and gas prices push the cost of most goods higher. Higher inflation usually leads to the Fed putting up interest rates.
- Interest rates, like inflation, are currently at historically low levels despite a recent hike. Obviously, they affect the rate at which companies can borrow. They may also depress the consumer sector if individuals find home loans too hard to pay at higher rates, or in the capital goods sector, if cash in the bank is earning a good rate of interest and business investment doesn't seem particularly attractive so that businesses don't invest. Equally, higher rates can lead to lower equity valuations (a *higher* earnings yield, remember, is equivalent to a *lower* price/earnings ratio).
- Non Farm Payrolls is an important number for gauging the U.S economy. It shows whether businesses are growing and need labor; it shows whether people are in employment and so able and willing to spend money. If there are labor shortages, that could impact labor-intensive services businesses.
- The Manufacturing PMI (Purchasing Managers' Index) shows whether the manufacturing sector is expanding (if PMI is over 50) or contracting (if PMI is under 50). There's also a Non-Manufacturing PMI which gives you data for the services sector. These indexes are made up of data on orders made, backlog, inventory changes, and they have proven to be quite useful in assessing the health of the corporate sector.

You can also find detailed data that can help with researching particular sectors. For instance, if you're investing in home builders or residential REITs, you'll want to look at building permits; if you own shares in Walmart, you'll want to follow month-by-month retail sales. Often, companies will show or refer to relevant economic data in their annual reports or (more often) in the analyst presentations, so when they do, make a note to add those series to your regular data feed.

A data series that a lot of investors used to see as a good lead indicator for global trade is the Baltic Dry Index (BDI). It measures the price of bulk shipping, which used to be a good proxy for trade flows. However, as global trade shifts from bulk commodities to container shipped manufactured goods, some observers feel the BDI isn't doing its job anymore.

Economic cycles and how they work

Knowing how economic cycles work is crucial to understanding cyclical sectors like energy and mining, chemicals and automobiles. While there's a powerful economic cycle that affects the top line of GDP, each industry sector also has its own cycle, and it works like this:

- Everyone needs a new XYZ. There's not enough XYZ to go around.
- The manufacturers of XYZ are making great profits, but they can't make enough XYZ to meet demand.
- So, they invest their profits in new XYZ capacity. All goes well for a while, until...
- Suddenly, there are too many new XYZs on the market. Prices go down and the manufacturers are making less money.
- Some of the manufacturers of XYZ go bust.
- Now, there aren't so many XYZs being made... and eventually, demand for XYZs increases again, and the price of an XYZ increases and the manufacturers who are left in the game are doing quite well.

- Which is great till they decide to invest in new XYZ capacity...
- And it all starts all over again.

Basically, the cycle works because capacity isn't scalable - you have to buy big chunks. You can't scale up a plant that will produce 250,000 cars a year by adding small increments to get another couple of percent production; you need to make a significant investment. So, the market tends to swing between periods of excess demand and periods of oversupply.

If you look at technology, semiconductors are a cyclical sector. Software, not so much - because adding new developers to the workforce isn't a chunky investment, but building a new fabrication plant is.

So, if you want to track a cyclical sector, you'll want to look at statistics for demand, supply, and pricing. For instance, Peter Lynch always looked at the price of second-hand automobiles as an indicator of the auto market - if the price went up, it was because there weren't enough vehicles available to meet demand, and this was usually the end of the cyclical trough and beginning of the upturn.

Many investors divide stocks into cyclical and defensive stocks. In this case, 'cyclical' doesn't always mean stocks that have an inherently cyclical nature, but stocks which respond very directly to economic activity.

Defensive stocks are those which tend to perform without regard to what the overall economy is doing - for instance, supermarkets, pharmaceuticals, and consumer staples such as cleaning products, tobacco, and Coca-Cola.

Generally, defensive stocks perform better during recessions, but will tend to underperform in a growth market when cyclical stocks will outperform. One thing I like to do is to look at GDP or consumer disposable income statistics compared with a company's revenues, to see if there's a relationship - it's easiest to do this visually, as you can see very easily if the two lines tend to run parallel or not.

There's also some evidence that particular sectors outperform in different stages of the economic cycle as a whole.

Expansion	Consumer discretionary stocks i.e. Televisions, cars
Peak	Metals, industrials, energy
Contraction	Healthcare, IT
Trough	Consumer staples, finance, utilities

Don't forget that the economic cycle could have a relatively small impact on revenues but a much more important impact on profits. That's particularly the case with businesses that have;

- high fixed costs (so they can't easily scale down),
- low margins (so any fall in price hurts them very hard),
- high borrowing costs (so when profits fall, the banks take much more of the profit).

You can also look at a stock's beta (the measure of its volatility, that is, how fast its price changes compared to changes in the market as a whole) as an indication of whether a stock is likely to be cyclical or defensive. Defensive stocks will have low betas (below 1).

It's quite difficult to see the exact relationship between the economic cycle in general and an individual company's profits in particular. But although it's difficult, it's well worth making the effort, as this can be an important factor in the performance of the stock over the medium term.

What's particularly interesting right now is that automotive, a cyclical industry, is also being affected by a major disruptive factor - the move to electric vehicles (EVs). All bets are off! That makes automotive higher risk than it was last time around since as well as betting on the cycle, you have to bet on which company will make the best transition to EVs.

How to 'test' economic data

Sometimes economic data doesn't tell you everything you want to know. For instance, inflation rates in 2021 appeared low - but in fact, the basket of goods typically bought by low-income households was getting much more expensive, much more quickly. Anyone trying to live on a low income could have told you about that... but the official data didn't.

In Russia in the 1990s, economic data and company figures looked good. But in 1998, Russia defaulted (failed to fulfil an obligation), and its stock market crashed. However, if you looked at a lot of companies' figures, you would have spotted that their return on capital was way lower than the bank interest rate, which meant that companies weren't earning high enough margins for it to be worth investing in.

These are two examples of the top line economic data not giving the whole picture, so I'd suggest if you want to do fundamental analysis properly, you find some other statistics that can let you 'test' the data.

In fact, in the first case, a new index called the Vimes Boots Index was created in the UK to show inflation for the lowest-cost staple foods (thanks to anti-poverty campaigner Jack Monroe and the estate of writer Terry Pratchett).

Goldman Sachs used to create an index of newspaper advertising as a check on economic growth - nowadays, you'd probably want to look at internet ads instead.

Wall Street analysts often carry out 'channel checking', for instance, ringing companies that are customers for capital goods to find out what they are buying, or checking retail stores to see which food companies are getting the most shelf space. Some have been known to pay for people to count the number of trucks visiting a factory.

You might also want to look at the spread between the interest rate on bonds and company returns on capital. Perhaps taking the largest stock in each sector in the S&P 100 to make this comparison would be a reasonable idea. Ideally, you'd want to re-run the figures every quarter to keep up with events.

Understanding economic impact on company results

Let's take a look at how the economy could affect a given company specifically.

- Interest rates - for an indebted company, a rise in interest rates could be very bad news. On the other hand, a company with strong cash generation and large cash reserves could add something to profits - though you probably wouldn't consider those earnings very high quality.

- Cost inputs - higher inflation might lead to significantly higher costs. In 2022, wind turbine manufacturers are facing a hike in their costs, and because they generally work on long term contracts (in which the delivered price has been set and is not adjustable), they're going to see their margins squeezed. On the other hand, some producers, such as those of luxury goods, are better able to pass on cost of inflation to their customers.

- Asset prices - for a real estate company, even one with a relatively well-structured balance sheet, a fall in asset prices could be a major concern. Banks often grant loans on the basis of a covenant which ensures the bank can call in the loan if it's not covered by a certain amount of assets. If the valuation of the properties in the company's portfolio falls, it may no longer be covered - and suddenly faces having to refinance or file for bankruptcy.

- Credit squeeze - a company which is burning cash may find it is unable to borrow to invest in its activities; companies with cash resources may take advantage in order to 'leapfrog' indebted rivals.

- High yield stocks may be downgraded if interest rates increase, as investors are able to get better yields from lower risk investments such as Treasuries.

Chapter 10 Quiz

1. Two major types of investing are;
    a. Bottom up and top down
    b. Forwards and backwards
    c. Straight and crooked
    d. Macroeconomic and macaroni

2. What are the phases of a cycle, in the right order?
    a. Expansion, peak, contraction, trough
    b. Contraction, peak, expansion, trough
    c. Trough, peak, expansion, contraction
    d. Invention, hype, bubble, crash

3. Which of these is not a way of testing economic data or company data?
    a. Creating your own index, for instance of food prices
    b. Relating the data to corporate results
    c. Visiting retail outlets to see what is selling
    d. Ordering the most expensive drink you can at Starbucks

4. What is a defensive stock?
    a. One with a big moat
    b. One whose results aren't much affected by economic change
    c. Boeing, General dynamics or Northrop Grumman
    d. One which has no foreign earnings

5. Why is the auto sector no longer a typical cyclical investment?
    a. There are not so many automotive manufacturers as there used to be
    b. No one buys cars anymore, they lease them
    c. It has been disrupted by the change to electric vehicles
    d. Mexico and Korea now have a big share of the market

11

Chapter 11: Defining 'buy' and 'sell'

Fundamental analysis is a tool, and it's a great tool. But it's not a commandment, and it won't answer the questions "Should I buy Tesla shares?" or "Should I sell Pfizer stock?". In that case, you might as well try asking your car where it would like to go this afternoon!

What you buy will not depend just on your analysis, either. It will also depend on your overall financial objectives. For instance, you may be driven by the desire to create a store of wealth through investing, or you may already have wealth but want to take an income from your investments. Even if you decide to invest in dividend paying stocks, you might decide to buy stocks with fast growing dividends and perhaps a lower yield or try to get the best yields you can, depending on your time horizon and need for funds.

Your decision will also depend on your particular risk appetite, whether you're more risk-averse or less. (When I was working a full-time job, I could afford to buy all-or-nothing tech stocks - now that I'm self-employed, I have to play things a bit safer.)

For instance, the 'dash for trash' as markets started recovering from the credit crunch saw some people investing in very highly indebted real estate companies. Basically, they were making a binary bet - one with only two outcomes - either that the company would go bust or that the share price would triple or quadruple. In fact, investors in many of these companies won their bet handsomely; but if you didn't like the amount of risk involved, you would have been right to stay out of the market.

However, while fundamental analysis won't tell you whether to buy or sell, it *will* tell you:

- whether the stock is vulnerable to particular external risks;
- whether the company is a good and growing business;
- the balance of risk and reward represented by the stock;
- whether the stock is trading at a cheap or expensive valuation.

That's all really useful information that you will use in making your decision.

Types of situations

As you gain experience, you'll probably find that there are particular types of situations where you do well. Let's take a look at these.

- Value, which can often involve buying the sector or company everybody hates. In 2003-4, it was technology, and in the 1990s, it was breweries. Right now, it seems to be biotech (unless the company has a COVID vaccine). If you find an out-of-favor sector selling at a significant discount to its intrinsic value, buy all the good quality stocks you can find. (It doesn't have to be *either* Pepsi *or* Coke - you can buy both if they both have the same attractions.) In simple words, an out-of-favor sector basically is a sector no one wants to buy, for whatever reason, and which is really undervalued.
- Turnaround. Sometimes you'll find a company which made a mis-step a few years ago, or where new management is expected to improve the business. If you can work out on the spreadsheet how the company can turn around within 18 months to 36 months and what it should be worth, then if it does, you may have a good investment. But remember, there is an execution risk.
- High growth. These stocks have driven the market for the last few years, and there's always an attractive story to go with the growth. The key is not to pay too much for that growth - and to have a good feeling about whether the growth forecast is realistic or way too optimistic. That's where high quality fundamental research will make all the difference to your investing.
- Dividend yielders. You could just buy the highest yielders in the index - but if you did, you'd end up with some real deadbeats. Your analysis will tell you if the company is paying a high yield because it's close to bankruptcy or because it's attractively valued (cheap as chips) with a strong cash flow.

- Misvaluations. This is where a business is valued in the wrong way. For instance, BAA, the owner of several British airports, was initially valued as a transportation stock. When it was looked at instead as a real estate stock, owning significant retail properties, it justified a price nearly three times higher. (Remember when you looked at Amazon's annual report and found out that it was a massive cloud services stock with a retailer attached? That's the kind of misunderstanding that creates this type of situation.)
- Cyclicals. If you get these stocks right, you can buy at just the right time in the cycle - before the business starts to turn around and when no one else wants the stock. Timing is crucial. You'll also need to have some way of averaging out earnings, as at the bottom of the cycle the price-earning ratio may look deceptively high on a single-year basis.
- Boring. Lots of people remember Peter Lynch buying retail and restaurant stocks like McDonald's, Home Depot, and Taco Bell. But he also loved buying stocks with really boring names and really boring businesses (though they were good quality) - because he found they were almost always overlooked by other investors.

You'll probably find out that your best deals come in two or three of these styles of investment. Concentrate on what you're good at, and keep working out what it was that tipped you off that these were the right stocks to buy. (I do well at misvaluations and turnarounds; I'm the world's worst investor in cyclicals, which somehow, I always get wrong.)

You may find that several of the stocks you like are trading very slightly above what you consider the right price. It's well worth setting an alert with your broker or on a finance website so that you are notified when the stock trades at the level you think is right to buy.

Recently, my friend built a position in French dividend payer Sanofi, a big pharmaceutical firm, buying when the dividend yield rose above 3.8%.

The first time he looked at it, he thought it was too expensive, but share price volatility had been his friend here, with the early 2020 Covid crash, then a vaccine failure story, helping him purchase it at a cheaper price.

Timing or value?

Timing an investment is difficult. If you spend your time looking at share price charts, you'll find it's never the right time to buy - either the shares have already gone up, so you feel you've 'missed' that amount of share price growth, or the shares are going down, so you worry that they'll carry on bleeding. Do you risk buying just before the results, or wait till afterwards?

Using your target price, set at a given percentage discount to the intrinsic value of the stock, spares you these uncertainties. The right time to buy a stock is whenever it's valued correctly. (Of course, if you're a growth investor, you might decide that buying the stock exactly at its intrinsic price is the right time, given that most growth stocks trade at a high valuation.)

You can build a stake gradually, buying whenever the price is right and you have money available. Unless the underlying fundamentals change, your target price remains the same. (Remember to check up on the tax treatment of gradual purchases and sales, which can differ depending on the jurisdiction within which you invest. And keep your records safe!)

Obviously, the right time to sell is when the shares are overvalued. You might decide that up to a 30% temporary overvaluation, you're not too worried - but above that level, you would want to take another look at the basics. It may be that the company has achieved growth and is now worth more - or it may be that the market has run away with enthusiasm, and the stock is trading too high. Don't decide to sell before you check which of these is the case!

If you always base your buying decisions on what you believe is the stock's real value, rather than on ideas of momentum or market timing, you'll make better decisions. And in fact, you are probably going to buy towards the bottom and sell towards the higher end of the range - even though you're not trying to 'time the market'.

Other times you might decide to sell

There are a few other times that you might decide to sell a stock. Let's run through those.

- When bad news undermines the entire basis of the valuation. For instance, if you buy a pharmaceutical stock and its main drug is found to be unsafe, or if you buy a mining exploration company and it doesn't find any mineral reserves, get out of it!
- When there is a major economic threat to the company's future, such as an interest rate hike when a company has high debts.
- One thing many brokers believe is that "profit warnings always come in threes". For the bigger, well-covered stocks, a major profit warning is unusual - analysts' expectations are usually well managed. So, a profit warning means not just that the company is underperforming, but that things worsened suddenly or that management didn't find out till it was too late. So, a hefty warning could be time to exit. However, a small underperformance wouldn't normally justify an exit.
- The resignation of the CEO or CFO is almost always time to go, particularly if it's coupled with a profit warning. When finance officers quit, it often means they have discovered something in the accounts that they didn't know was there, and it is *never* good news. If there are also other signs of poor governance (such as large related party transactions) that would confirm your decision to exit.

- Slow but steady deterioration in the growth rate, in the company's financial strength, margins, or cash flow - particularly if the company is in denial rather than actively trying to improve matters.
- A cut in the dividend may mean it's time to quit, particularly if the yield is one of the main reasons for buying a stock. However, it's not always the case - some companies decided to cut their dividend in 2020 because they wanted to retain more margin if the pandemic damaged their business and then reinstated the dividend later on. But if a dividend cut accompanies some signs of deterioration or financial stress, it is usually a sign that something is wrong.
- Increasing risk. If a company is beginning to lose its 'moat', if new and well-funded rivals have entered the market, or if the company's major foreign market sees a regime change which could imperil its earnings, those are all examples of increased risk. The valuation should reflect that higher risk - you would want to buy at a higher discount to the intrinsic value. But this wouldn't necessarily justify an immediate sale.

You might also want to sell because you've changed your investment strategy. For instance, if you decide to prioritize regular income rather than capital growth, you might want to sell the companies that are not paying a dividend. Or, of course, you may simply need to cash out some of your stock position to raise cash if you're buying a house or taking a sabbatical.

While fundamental analysts generally ignore what the share price is doing in the market, I'd like to suggest that there's one time that you shouldn't do that. This is when the share price falls very significantly for no apparent reason. I don't mean a 3% fall - I mean something of the order of 15% or 20% over just a couple of days. I have found through experience that that is often the first sign of something very bad - perhaps fraud or a series of profit warnings.

So, if I see a stock fall far and fast, the first thing I do is check out why. Sometimes I can explain it easily; an earnings miss, a change to guidance, or a competitor spreading bad news. A failed clinical trial, or a contract that the company saw go to a rival, could also explain a sudden fall in the share price.

But if there seems to be no reason, you might be best taking a loss and making your exit.

Chapter 11 Quiz

1. Which of these is not a type of stock situation you might invest in?
   a. Turnaround
   b. Value
   c. Cyclical
   d. Titanic

2. Which of these should not affect your purchase decision for a stock?
   a. Your investment objectives
   b. The stock's valuation
   c. Past share price performance
   d. The company's past performance

3. Which of these is not a possible reason for selling a stock?
   a. Steady deterioration in financial ratios
   b. Sudden resignation of the CFO
   c. A single negative earnings surprise
   d. A big cut in the dividend

4. If you are highly risk averse, and you refused to buy a stock because it had a 50% risk of going bankrupt, and it subsequently doubled in price, you made;
   a. A stupid decision
   b. A good decision
   c. A bad decision
   d. A mathematically incorrect decision

5. Traditionally, profit warnings always come in;
   a. June
   b. The last quarter
   c. Hot weather
   d. Threes

12

Chapter 12: The best of both worlds - combining FA and TA

Fundamental analysis (FA) and technical analysis (TA) would seem to be two very different, even mutually exclusive, approaches to the stock market.

Fundamental analysis says that a stock has an intrinsic value, however volatile the market price might be, and that the intrinsic value is based on the activities and profitability of the underlying business.

Technical analysis says that a stock is worth what someone is willing to pay you for it and aims to predict share price movements by analyzing supply and demand patterns (usually graphically, which is why technical analysis is also known as 'charting').

Fundamental Analysis for Beginners

In fact, though the two approaches are based on very different theories, they are not necessarily incompatible. To use them together, you need to understand what each approach is intended to do and what sort of decision it is best used for.

- Technical analysis tends to look at short and medium term trends, while fundamental analysis looks at the long term value of a stock.
- Technical analysis considers the stock price as the outcome of market trading activity, whereas fundamental analysis considers it as a representation of the value of the company.

Every share has this dual nature - it is both a share in a real business and a financial instrument that can be traded. If you can sell a share in a business that you believe is actually worth nothing to the market at $25, what is the "right" price - zero or $25?

A share price chart is a graphical way of assessing the balance of positive and negative emotions in the market - traders who are greedy, traders who are afraid, buyers and sellers, supply and demand. It is a summary of market behavior. It doesn't say whether that behavior was sensible or stupid, it doesn't say why traders made the trades they did - it simply sums up the facts.

So technical analysis can be useful in looking at timing. And fundamental analysis can be useful for a technical trader in giving a bit more background to the share price movements. Although I'm a long term investor for a lot of my wealth, I run part of my portfolio as a trading book and use technical analysis to trade, with some success. I'm quite realistic about the two approaches: I noticed that my technical trades had a lower failure rate when I got to understand fundamentals, and I know that as a long term investor, I can use technical analysis to show me when I'm likely to get a lower in-price if I wait a bit.

A.Z Penn

Some technical analysis basics

Technical analysis got started when Charles Dow (the same Dow who invented the Dow Jones index) created the Dow Theory. His theory was that despite all the 'noise' of daily price changes, stock markets move in trends, which are relatively predictable, and continue till a definite signal ends the trend. He sees the trend as similar to an economic cycle - it begins with an accumulation phase in which traders start buying, moves into a public participation phase in which the stock becomes popular, and ends in a panic phase (speculative bubble), ending in a crash.

He also stressed the need for confirmation; in a major trend, all the relevant indices should confirm each other by moving in the same direction, and trading volumes should also confirm the trend. So, for instance, the S&P 100, S&P 500, DJIA, and Nasdaq Composite should all be moving in the same direction if the U.S market is trending upwards. If one of them isn't, something is wrong, or the trend is weak.

Since then, technical analysis has developed into a major investment discipline. It has been particularly helped by the availability of technology that made charts easily available first via services such as Reuters and Bloomberg to Wall Street firms and then through the internet to individual investors. In Dow's day, you had to draw your own charts with paper and pencil.

Technical analysis relies on pattern recognition. Certain types of market behavior recur frequently - like booms, bubbles and crashes, but on a micro scale - technical analysis aims to spot the patterns that lead to price movements and then see where current share prices are going. It's worth pointing out that these patterns are fractal (they repeat in ever small versions) - Dow might have looked at a pattern over a number of years, but you can find exactly the same pattern occurring within a single afternoon's trading.

These patterns are generated by investor behavior, which tends to follow particular habits. For instance, investors often jump into a stock when it makes the news, and so they have all bought at about the same price. And because the human brain works this way, even though the price they bought at isn't necessarily the intrinsic price (as fundamental analysis defines it), that's the price they remember. So, if the share price goes up and then comes down, they will get very fearful when it gets close to the price at which they bought it. If it goes up again, they'll stay in and maybe buy some more - if it goes down further, they may panic and sell out. That creates zones of what's called support and resistance around particular price levels.

Often, it will create a price range within which the share trades fairly reliably up and down between the support line (at the bottom) and the resistance line (at the top). Sometimes, you'll find that support and resistance relate to fundamental data - the resistance might be roughly where the share's dividend yield falls below the average yield on the S&P 500, and the stock, therefore, becomes less attractive to income investors.

Say a stock pays a $2 dividend and is priced at $50; that's a 4% yield ($2 / $50). It's not very attractive, and if there's no other great reason to buy the stock, then the price could drift down. But as it gets towards $33, it's getting towards a 6% yield ($2 / $33), and that's very attractive if we think the dividend is safe. So, about that level, buyers will emerge, and that will probably push the price up again. But with the price pushing up, the yield will fall again, and the stock will sell off again.

Chartists (technical analysts) will often draw lines across the chart, linking up all the highest highs and all the lowest lows. This might show a horizontal channel, or it might show share prices trading within a diagonal channel, in an uptrend, or in a downtrend. Most good chart websites let you draw your own lines over the charts on the computer screen by dragging and dropping with the mouse. I find that a good way of analyzing the trends.

While as a long term investor you're not going to be trading the range (that is, buying towards the bottom and selling at the top), it's useful to know if a stock has set up a trading range. If you are looking to add to your positions in a stock you hold, when the price is in the bottom decile of the range, it's obviously a good time to buy. So here, you would use technical analysis to help your timing and maybe get a 5-10% discount on your purchase.

Most traders concentrate on **breakouts** when a stock price shoots through a support or resistance line. Traders will try to buy in really quickly and ride the breakout to a profit. However, as a fundamental analyst, that's not why you should be interested in breakouts. You should be interested because a strong breakout shows you that something is happening. An upside breakout could mean the market is reacting well to results, a new product, or some other good news, or it could mean a couple of major investors are buying in. On the other hand, a downside breakout (or breakdown) could mean there is bad news on the way. Be very cautious about breakdowns - particularly if you have begun to worry about a stock's high valuation or about an area of its business performance.

Technical analysis indicators

Technical analysis indicators take the price data and perform various mathematical operations, such as creating an additional chart line that can give you extra information. For instance, moving averages aim to smooth out short term fluctuations in the share price to give you a better idea of the trend.

You don't need to know all the kinds of technical indicators - On balance volume, oscillators, aroon indicators, accumulation/distribution lines, and stochastics. However, there are a few indicators that I think you ought to be acquainted with, as they can give you useful information.

Moving averages (MA) are a good place to start. The share price movement is averaged out over a certain period. Technical analysts often like shorter term averages, but as a fundamental investor, it's probably best to look at the longer term moving averages, for instance, 50 and 200 days.

The 'golden cross' (and its opposite the 'death cross') is a particularly strong indicator that I find helpful. When the shorter term average crosses over the longer term average, it tells you that the trend is reversing. When you're using two relatively long term averages, it's not likely to be a short term blip. So, if I've already identified a stock as one I want to buy, and I see a 'golden cross', with the shorter term average crossing from below to above the longer one, then I think this is a good time to buy the stock. I'm not going to hang around!

Equally, if I've seen a few things that make me feel worried about the stock, or I have a feeling that the stock is getting overvalued, and I see a 'death cross', that might be the nudge I need to act on my concerns and sell at least part of my holding. Seeing this pattern emerge when I'm already losing money is also a potential warning to cut my losses - unless I'm a hundred percent sure of my analysis.

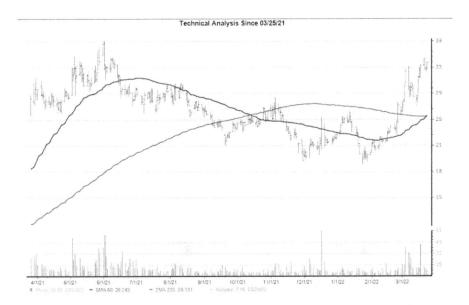

Technical Analysis Since 03/25/21

In the chart above, you see an example of the Olympic Steel stock. (Its ticker symbol is Zeus, which I found really clever!). You'll see that there was a death cross at the end of October 2021. The 50-day MA red line went below the long 200-day MA green line. But you can also see that it's forming a golden cross right about today!

Bollinger bands are another useful indicator. To explain them, I do need to get into a slightly nerdy area of statistics, though you don't need to understand stats to make use of the bands. Bollinger bands are plotted one standard deviation away from the moving average line.

What's a standard deviation? It's a measurement of how dispersed a set of data is. For instance, if you look at how big different breeds of dog are, they go from chihuahuas all the way up to English Mastiff, but probably most dogs are around the size of a labrador retriever or vizsla. The standard deviation is a measure of 'normal'. Usually, it covers nearly 70% of the relevant data.

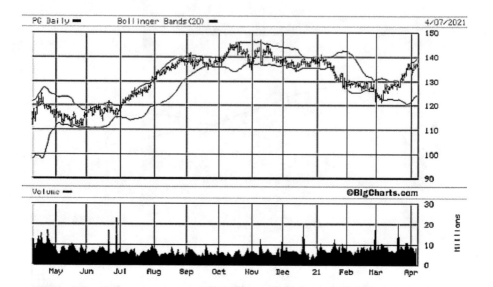

If you draw a line one standard deviation above and one standard deviation below the mean, so it makes a solid band. Then chihuahuas are below it, English Mastiff above it, and most breeds will end up somewhere within the band.

Back to Bollinger bands. They show how dispersed prices are, how much prices are going up and down - they show volatility. When they are wide, they show that the share price is moving around a lot. When they tighten, that shows share prices are tending to trade around quite a concentrated area. Now, this wouldn't normally be very useful to know, but there are a couple of times that the bands show a message;

- when the bands tighten significantly, it's likely that the price will break out in one direction or the other;
- when the price breaks out of the bands and keeps moving in the direction of the breakout, you can expect that trend to continue.

However, normally you wouldn't use the bands as your lead indicator - you'd look at the bands to confirm a signal from the other indicators (support line, resistance line, golden cross).

Volume

Share price charts intended for use by technical analysts almost always show an indicator of the volume of shares traded at the bottom. That's important because it tells you how seriously to take a share price move.

If, for instance, there's not much interest in the stock, and it falls 5% on a single trade, you wouldn't take that too seriously. But if it falls 5% *and* there's a lot of volume, that means a significant number of investors have decided to sell. You'd take that a lot more seriously.

It's also interesting to note that a crash in the market or in a single share's price is often followed by a period of very low volume. Investors who got their fingers burned are staying out of the way.

And of course, if you remember Dow Theory, trends are confirmed by volume… so this aspect of markets has been recognized for over a hundred years.

Other ways to use charts

One thing that charts show very clearly, whereas numbers on a page might not, is momentum. When a share price starts going up more quickly than before, you immediately notice that the curve becomes steeper.

As a fundamental analyst, you're not interested in share price momentum. But if you use your spreadsheet charting function to put a company's financial data in chart form, you may find you can see trends more clearly than simply looking at the numbers. I find that a quarterly revenue chart is really helpful in seeing whether a company is gaining traction or slipping behind. I also like to chart net income per share. It's really easy to see acceleration or deceleration in growth.

I also like to compare the price charts of different companies in the same sector. For instance, I want to look at Ford, GM and Stellantis together. That shows me clearly if one of the companies is out of step with the rest of its sector. I may know why - or I might want to see if I can find out. That's useful information, though, as so often, it's just a pointer to the need to do a bit more research rather than telling me whether or not the stock should be bought.

Before we end this chapter, just so you know, in my free bonus #2 – Charting Simplified Masterclass I share various technical analysis strategies which can help you determine whether it's the right time to buy a stock. I highly recommend you visit www.az-penn.com to watch the 5-part video masterclass.

Chapter 12 Quiz

1. What is resistance?
   a. When a company won't accept a takeover bid
   b. A level above which the share price does not rise
   c. A level below which the share price does not sink
   d. Resistance is useless

2. Bollinger bands are
   a. Labels on champagne bottles
   b. Drawn one standard deviation around the moving average
   c. Lines showing the support and resistance levels
   d. Always based on the 30 day moving average

3. The golden cross and death cross occurs when
   a. A short term moving average crosses a longer term moving average
   b. The moving average crosses the support line
   c. The moving average crosses the resistance line
   d. The Bollinger bands tighten around the moving average

4. What is a breakout?
   a. When a stock price breaks through a trendline
   b. When a stock price jumps suddenly
   c. When a stock price breaks through a support or resistance line
   d. When the moving average changes direction

5. The underlying premise of technical analysis is that
   a. Investor psychology creates behavior that is predictable
   b. Stock prices are a self-fulfilling prophecy
   c. The stock market is totally unpredictable
   d. Investors are all stupid

13

Chapter 13: Top tips

Five top tips for analyzing the quality of a business the MBA way

Although fundamental analysis is often put forward as just a quantitative way to analyze stocks, you'll really benefit by applying a few business school-style approaches too.

1. SWOT analysis

Draw a box and divide it into four quarters. Label the quarters: Strengths, Weaknesses, Opportunities, Threats.

Now, look at the company and fill in the factors that you see affecting its prospects.

For Amazon, strengths would include market share, brand name, IT infrastructure, and international operations.

For weaknesses, I think going into bricks and mortar stores is a big, big, big mistake. I think they have a great business model for delivered goods, and it works partly because their real estate costs are inexpensive. But also, search engines and algorithms work in e-commerce - I'm not sure they would in groceries.

Opportunities might include international expansion, backward integration, and moving into new product areas - for instance, business-to-business goods.

Threats would include significant bricks-and-mortar retailers moving into e-commerce or government regulation.

SWOT Analysis

Strengths	Weaknesses
Opportunities	Threats

2. Growth/share matrix

This is another four-box grid with two axes - low to high growth and low to high share.

You can look at companies or individual products this way, placing each company or each product on the growth and market share axes.

'Stars' are products that have high share and high growth - they're great news for you as an investor.

'Cash cows' have high share but low growth - also good news.

'Questions marks' have low share and high growth, they might be interesting but are high risk, so don't bother.

'Dogs' have low growth coupled with low market share - this is a very weak place to be so don't bother investing in them!

Where would you put Amazon?

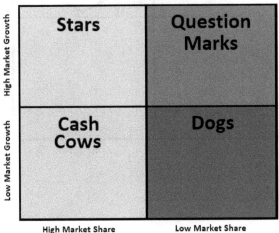

Growth/Share Matrix

3. Strategic group analysis

This is a free-form way of looking at a sector by taking particular strategies or characteristics and seeing which companies belong to which group.

For instance, you might look at which companies are taking a lowest-cost approach to the sector and which are taking a full-service (higher-cost) approach. Then you can see where the most successful companies belong.

You can look at outsourced vs own-production; direct sale to end users vs using a distributor network; market segmentation (e.g. teenager-focused products vs the market for seniors) - any way you can slice up the sector.

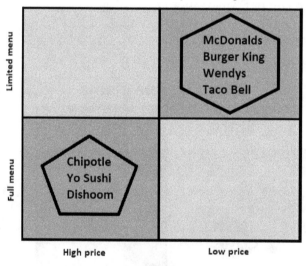

4. Porter's Five Forces

This is a way of looking at a company's power within its industry ecosystem.

The five forces are existing rivals, potential new rivals, suppliers, buyers, and substitute products or services.

So, for Amazon, you might have eBay as an existing rival, Walmart as a potential new rival, publishers and IT hardware companies as suppliers, consumers, and cloud computing users as buyers.

You then need to look at the strength of rivals, suppliers, and buyers.

Individual consumers don't have much power, nor do Amazon's suppliers.

It is rivals who are likely to do the most damage.

5. PEST (or STEP) analysis

This covers political, economic, social and technological factors affecting the company.

Amazon has plenty of political factors, from "does it pay enough tax?" to monopoly and anti-trust issues.

Economic factors would be household disposable income (going up or down?) or cost of distribution (big hike in fuel tax or prices might be an issue).

Social factors would be growing internet-aware population and emergence of influencers on Instagram and TikTok.

Technology factors include the move to cloud computing, increased storage requirements, and Amazon's search ranking algorithms.

Pest Analysis

Political Factors	Economic Factors
Social Factors	Technological Factors

Ten top tips for becoming a successful fundamental investor

1. Do the work! Don't skimp on learning about annual reports and spreadsheets or reading up on industries. Fundamental analysis takes time, though that time will be well rewarded.

2. Diversify. If you're a doctor, the temptation might be to buy only healthcare stocks. You have an advantage there, right? But you should diversify to protect yourself from surprises. Hold stocks in different sectors, and aim to build a portfolio with between 10 and 20 stocks.

3. There is no either/or. People often ask, "which stock should I buy in this sector?" That's dumb. You can buy all the stocks in that sector that look like great businesses at a good price - though you should remember that you *will* need the time to keep up to date with all those companies.

4. Develop your instinct. Every time you say something like "I don't trust this," or "hey, this could be interesting", note it down. How did your gut feeling work out? If you regularly go back and check, you'll work out why you had that feeling, and you'll be refining your ability to pick up those tiny clues.

5. Reinvest, reinvest, reinvest. If you don't need the dividends you're paid for as income, reinvest them, whether in the company that paid them or in another company. If one of your stocks gets taken over, look for somewhere else to invest that money. If you have money left over at the end of the month, buy some more stock in one of the companies you hold. Over the long term, all these additional purchases will create a much higher return for your portfolio.

6. Read deeply rather than listening to superficial news. If you have a choice between watching CNBC and watching The Big Short or between reading a newspaper and reading an in-depth report on cloud computing or sustainable energy technologies, go for the in-depth report.

7. Don't watch stock prices too closely. Yes, you need to monitor your portfolio, but don't keep dialing up your share prices every half an hour. Spend the time on reading the company's financial statements and keeping up to date on its industry, instead.

8. Don't be in a hurry. Fear of Missing Out (FOMO) is a big driver for some investors. But if you're buying a stock for long term growth, you don't need to worry about missing a week or two - do your work properly before you make the decision.
9. Never take a stock tip. Not from the taxi driver, not from the guy at Starbucks, not from Reddit, not from someone you meet at a party, not from your best friend. Do your own research and make your own decisions.
10. Learn what you're best at. If it's not fundamental analysis, buy index funds. If it's growth stocks, buy growth stocks. If it's turnarounds, go look for turnarounds. And conversely, if your failure rate on high yield stocks is 100%, find something else for your portfolio.

Top tips for getting the best out of fundamental analysis

1. If you're a very visual person, run all your data series as charts. You'll spot trends much more quickly this way.
2. Find which ratios 'say' the most to you, and concentrate on those.
3. Always keep a written record of the reasons you bought (or sold) a stock.
4. Monitor your decisions. Take a weekend every six months when you can sit down and assess your decisions - the good ones, the bad ones, and 'the ones that got away'.
5. Read a major analyst's report at least every three months. Sector reports and IPO analyses are often the best, as they go into real detail. Take notes, and be prepared to criticize.
6. Keep a record of stocks you decided *not* to buy. Revisiting those decisions is always interesting.
7. Build your own templates and questionnaires for assessing companies, and use them every time you look at a new company.
8. Have good sources *outside* the stock market - such as trade journals, product reviews, industry bloggers, and people who buy and use the products your companies make.
9. Understand that your needs and resources will change over time. If you launch a new business, your portfolio may need to change if you don't have the time to spend on it.
10. Never invest money that you need in the short term or can't afford to lose. If you sometimes have difficulty paying the rent, the stock market is not for you - at least, not yet.

Top questions to answer before you buy a stock

1. What is the quality of the company's earnings?
2. Does the company have a defensible 'moat'?
3. Can the company manage its debt?
4. Is it generating good cash flow?
5. Does management have a track record of delivering on promises?
6. Is the industry undergoing disruptive change? If so, is the company a winner or loser?
7. Where is the saturation point for the company's service/ product?
8. Who are the main competitors?
9. What are the top five risks facing the company?
10. What events would make me decide to sell the stock?

I would just like to mention before we go onto the final chapter on building your portfolio, if you are finding this book useful so far – it would mean everything to me if you could spare just a few seconds and <u>write a brief review on Amazon</u> on how this book is helping you so far.

14

Chapter 14: Build a portfolio

So far, this book has been about how to do fundamental analysis. Now, I'm going to turn to a more general investment topic - building a portfolio.

If you don't use fundamental analysis to build a portfolio of investments, it's not been worth your time unless you're actually going to put some money into the companies! (Or if you're getting paid for it as a professional analyst).

The first step on the way is identifying stocks that might be worth analyzing and also cutting out the stocks that aren't worth your time. There are a good few approaches that can help. One is simply looking up any company whose service, products or strategy you've come across and that strikes you as high quality, innovative, or interesting.

Another is to screen for stocks that fit your criteria, using sites like Finviz, Morningstar, MSN Money, Reuters or Zacks.

You might use a positive screening approach to look for companies which, for example, have a return on equity (ROE) above the S&P 500 average (currently 18%), or above the average for a particular sector.

For your information, I've shown a select few sectors in the table on the next page. You can get the lot, up to date, by pulling up the data on Aswath Damodaran's website.

Fundamental Analysis for Beginners

Sector	ROE %
Aerospace and defense	9.1
Alcoholic beverages	4.4
Pharmaceutical	14.6
Homebuilding	27.4
Oil and gas (integrated)	1.2
Water utility	10.4
Software (system and application)	30.5
Retail (general)	20.1
Retail (online)	44.1

Source: Aswath Damodaran at: http://pages.stern.nyu.edu/~adamodar

You might look for companies with a growth rate above 10%, companies with no net debt or companies above or below a certain size.

You can create quite a complex screening; for instance, companies with a dividend yield above 3%, excluding oils and financials, and with dividend cover of 1.5 or more, and earnings growth above 8%.

That doesn't mean every stock you find that ticks those boxes is a buy, but if you are a dividend investor who wants both security and growth, you will find stocks that are worth spending a bit more time analyzing.

You can also take a negative approach, screening out companies that don't fit certain criteria. For instance, I sometimes run a screen that works on the following exclusions:

- no loss-makers (i.e. net income >0),
- no non dividend paying stocks,
- no stocks below $50m market capitalization,
- no stocks with a price/earning more than 10% above the market (overall or by sector).

I then add a couple of extra steps that stock screeners can't help me with. I look up any bonds issued by the company, and if they don't have an investment grade rating, I chuck the company out. And I look to see if there's a Dividend Reinvestment Program (DRIP) and prioritize research on stocks that have one. It's an easy way to make sure that my money is reinvested, rather than having cash sitting in my brokerage account which I need to think about reinvesting, and there's often a discount.

I now also have a rule that says "no bargain basement stocks." I am quite good at buying undervalued stocks, and I am quite good at buying high yielders. But every so often, I get suckered into buying a deadbeat stock because it looks really, really cheap. I now screen out stocks that have a yield *more* than three times that of the market. It's possible - but not likely - that this will mean I miss a real bargain, but it stops me from wasting time on junk.

Your system might be different. This one works for me because I want income, and I want value stocks. But it doesn't always give me stocks with great growth prospects.

Sometimes, I miss a good turnaround stock because the 'no lossmakers' rule excludes the company that had a big exceptional loss last year, as well as the no-hope start-up stocks.

Before you start screening, it's worth brainstorming what you're looking for in a stock.

Diversification

You could just screen, analyze the stocks, find the stocks you think are worth buying, and buy them. But that's not building a portfolio any more than going out and buying pictures you like is 'art collecting'. To build a proper portfolio, you must consider asset allocation and diversification.

Asset allocation is a way of looking at investments in terms of what kinds of assets (bonds, real estate, stocks) or what kind of stocks (value, growth, different sectors or geographies) you own. Most brokers will show you your allocation via a pie chart according to sector and geographical split, which can help you get a feel for how you're doing in terms of diversification.

Why diversify? Because bad things happen. There are two kinds of bad things that can happen - the company can do badly, or the whole market can do badly. If the stock market crashes or the whole economy goes into recession, that's *system risk* - it's a risk you can't do anything about. If you're invested at all, you run that risk. But if a company loses a big lawsuit, loses a contract to a competitor, or launches a new product that fails, that's a *specific risk* which affects only that company.

In order to reduce the amount of specific risk that you run, you can simply buy a number of stocks with different characteristics, for instance, in different sectors. If one of them stumbles, the others should keep your portfolio on track.

Diversification doesn't just mean having 10-20 stocks. It means you don't want to buy only consumer stocks or only banks or only REITs. You might emphasize one sector a bit more than other investors, but you should always have some backup - either in terms of other stocks or by placing a portion of your portfolio in an index fund or in mutual funds.

You also need to think about how much each stock should represent in your portfolio. To start with, you might say you'll put $500 into each stock and over a year, aim to invest in ten stocks. That's not a bad plan. But if one of your stocks really takes off, you could end up in a few years' time with one holding that's worth nearly half your entire portfolio.

That's why I suggest *rebalancing*. You do that by selling some of the best performer - not all of it because you're in this for the long term - and investing the money in the other stocks (as long as the fundamentals are still intact). I don't like any stock to get to more than 20% of my total investment. So, I sell off the top a little and rebalance. The amount I do that will vary depending on the valuation - if a stock has done well because the company has hugely improved its performance, I will sell off less, but if the company is getting highly valued, I might sell off a little more.

But never sell completely out of an investment that is doing well unless its valuation has become unsustainable. Individual investors often keep stocks that are losing them money (because no one likes to materialize a loss) and sell their best performers because they get nervous about the share price. Peter Lynch calls this "cutting down the flowers and watering the weeds". If you got your analysis right at the beginning and the company continues to grow, stay in there - just make sure you don't have your entire portfolio in one or two stocks.

Incidentally, buying more and more stocks isn't worth it for diversification. An academic study worked out that 20 stocks should be enough to diversify, and adding more stocks doesn't reduce risk by very much at all.

Many investors in tech stocks were sitting on millions in 1999 - and lost almost everything in 2000. By diversifying and rebalancing every six months or so, you should ensure that you never risk your whole portfolio. You can sleep easy at night. Isn't that what we all want?

Watch out for red flags.

The magic of compounding most of the time works for you as an investor. For instance, if you start investing in your pension fund when you're 20, you'll end up with a vast amount more in it than if you start investing when you're 40, even if at that age you have more to invest. If you stay invested in the stock market and reinvest dividends and profits, you'll end up with more than if you skip in and out of stocks.

But compounding works *against* you if you lose money. If a stock's price halves, it has to *double* before you get back the money. That's a big ask. So, the big rule of how to make money is: **don't lose money.**

That's why you need to have a list of red flags. There are more than enough investments in the world - there must be more than 20 stocks in the S&P 500 that are worth buying, right?

So, I suggest that when you come across the red flag, you don't go any further with your analysis - just walk. Better opportunities will come along.

- The company has problems getting paid. If it's making the sales, but it has 365 Days Sales Outstanding, it's junk.
- Big write-offs every year. Write-offs are like "the dog ate my homework": it might be true once, but if the same excuse gets trotted out two or three times, you know it's just an excuse.
- Cash flow is much lower than profit. This is a big red flag. It might happen one year, with a big investment, but if it happens two or three times, the company has a problem.
- Debt keeps increasing. Something is not right here if the company appears to be making money, but it keeps increasing debt every year. Unless it's making a lot of acquisitions, which would explain the debt, you should keep away.
- 'Black box' technology. If the company can't explain how it makes its money, avoid it. (Two or three major investors asked Bernie Madoff how his fund made so much money. They didn't think his answer made sense. Bernie defrauded many investors because they would invest in something they couldn't understand. However, these investors didn't fall for his line - and they kept their money out of his fund. If you try and try and just can't work out how a business makes money, then... stay away! Those investors spared themselves a lot of hassle.)
- Bubble valuations. Even if you're a growth investor, paying the price/earning multiples of 50, 60, and upwards is risky. If a highly valued share disappoints the market, its price can tumble fast. On the other hand, if a share on a low multiple has good results, sometimes the effect can be like your neighbor's no-good dumb teenager coming home with a job offer - even if it's working as a burger flipper, he's done great!
- Valuation mini-bubbles in particular sectors. In the 1970s, the Nifty Fifty were 'buy and hold forever' stocks; big, 'safe' companies. The only trouble was they were valued way too high. Result: they crashed. In 1979-80 the Hunt brothers tried to corner the market in silver; the silver price rose from $11 to $50 - and then crashed. The late 1990s saw the tech bubble - and crash; 2004-6 saw the sub-prime mortgage sector supporting high valuations for homes and home builders - and a subsequent crash.

Fundamental Analysis for Beginners

Remember that economist JM Keynes said, "the stock market can stay irrational longer than you can stay solvent." So don't lose money, don't bet the bank, and don't risk money you need to live on or pay the rent. However sure you are of your research; you *can* be wrong. (Or you can be right about the fantastic business, but the stock market can carry on ignoring the stock for years.)

I'm also wary of IPOs (initial public offerings). Sometimes they will do well. Sometimes not. But there's often a lot of hoopla around an IPO, together with a lot of behind-the-scenes bargaining going on. They can be very disappointing, particularly when they are trying to take advantage of a valuation mini-bubble. Aircraft leasing company GPA didn't manage to raise the funds it needed - a few years later, it went bust. Uber expected $120bn for its IPO but kept cutting its target and eventually only raised $69bn. Pets.com, Etsy, and Webvan had IPOs that lost money - Etsy is actually a great business, but the shares initially fell from the $16 IPO price to $6.90 (now they're trading at $116).

As for SPACs (Special Purpose Acquisition Companies), which are formed to raise money in order to make acquisitions, you should ask yourself how you can do fundamental analysis on a company that doesn't actually have a business. SPACs are a pure gamble.

I'm also wary of stocks with no earnings. Just occasionally, a loss maker is worth buying. For instance, a company in a mature sector that has had a single disastrous year could be worth buying for a turnaround. But for the most part, if a company hasn't broken into profit, it's too early for it to be on the stock market. You need to be super sure of your analysis and very clear about how (and when) the business is going to make a profit to get involved.

Chapter 14 Quiz

1. Diversification will;
    a. Stop you ever losing money
    b. Reduce the total risk of your portfolio
    c. Reduce the risk of individual stocks
    d. Not make much difference to any of the above

2. Stock screening is useful because;
    a. You can use it to pick the right investments
    b. You can pick stocks which conform to your investment requirements
    c. It will find undervalued stocks for you
    d. It can help you avoid fraudulent companies

3. Which of these is not a red flag?
    a. 'Black box' technology
    b. Big write-offs every year
    c. Ever-increasing debt
    d. An annual report printed on pink paper

4. Warren Buffett is fond of saying, "The first rule of investment is don't lose money." What is the second rule?
    a. No one talks about Investment Club.
    b. Only invest in big-moat stocks.
    c. Remember rule one.
    d. Keep cash in the bank.

5. Why is portfolio rebalancing a good idea?
    a. Because different stock performances could leave your portfolio poorly diversified
    b. Because last year's top stock will always be next year's dog
    c. Because you should always keep exactly the same percentage in each stock
    d. Because it gives you something to do

Fundamental Analysis for Beginners

Leave a 1-Click Review!

I would be incredible thankful if you could take just 60 seconds to write a brief review on Amazon, even if it's just a few sentences!

Customer reviews

⭐⭐⭐⭐⭐ 5 out of 5

4 global ratings

5 star	████████	100%
4 star		0%
3 star		0%
2 star		0%
1 star		0%

˅ How are ratings calculated?

Amazon.com readers
http://www.amazon.com/review/
create-review?&asin=B0B9QWF9ZJ

Amazon.co.uk readers
http://www.amazon.co.uk/review/
create-review?&asin=B0B9QWF9ZJ

Conclusion

If you've read this far, you've got a good idea of the basics of fundamental analysis. All you need to do is go and practice with some real live companies.

You know that fundamental analysis means looking at the business underneath the shares. You've learned how to read an annual report and how to calculate the basic ratios, which will let you interpret those pages of figures to find out what's really happening in the business. You know how to look at an industry and what kinds of information can be useful in assessing a business's quality and growth prospects. You also know several ways to value a business.

That's really all you need to be able to start looking for profitable investments in the stock market. I can't promise you an immediate profit - no one can - but I *can* promise that if you get your analysis right and make sensible investment decisions to build a portfolio, over the long term, your investments should perform well for you. I can also promise that you know how to avoid the most typical mistakes that lose investors money, which is something worth knowing!

I've also introduced you to technical analysis - just enough to be able to look at a share price chart as more than a pretty picture. If you find it useful as I do, you'll find it's easy to integrate with your fundamentals-driven approach; if you don't, concentrate on the fundamentals and ignore the charts.

There are two words in this book that should now be engraved on the inside of your skull; **valuation** and **risk**. Interestingly enough, they're two words you hardly ever hear on financial TV, except in relation to the market as a whole. When was the last time you heard someone talk about the risk/reward ratio for real estate investment or the valuation of Walmart?

It's because you know about valuation and risk and because you know how to quantify them that you're now streets ahead of other rookie investors. They'll be buying a story - you are buying a business. They'll be buying hope - you'll be buying fact.

I hope you've enjoyed this book and that it's taught you some valuable lessons for your future investing success. I'm always interested to find out what my readers think, so if you can, please leave a review on Amazon! Or if you enjoyed it, I'll be really glad to find out. Just *don't* try to give me any stock tips!

A.Z Penn

HOW TO GET THE MOST OUT OF THIS BOOK

To help you along your investing journey, I've created two free bonus companion masterclasses, one which includes walking you through an investors mindset on how to find potential companies to invest in. There's also a free companion DCF model spreadsheet of Amazon which I created specifically to simplify your learning of this valuation model. I also provide an additional colored images resource that will help you get the best possible result.

I highly recommend you sign up now to get the most out of this book. You can do that by visiting the link or scanning the QR code below:

www.az-penn.com

Free bonus #1: Company Valuation Simplified Masterclass ($97 value)

In this video masterclass, I will be walking you through an investors mindset on how to find potential companies to invest in, which includes what to look out for and major red flags to keep in mind. This class will help you decide whether a company is worth investing in or whether you should move on.

Free bonus #2: **Charting Simplified Masterclass ($67 value)**

In this 5 part video masterclass you'll be discovering various simple and easy to use strategies on making profitable trades. By showing you real life stock examples of a few charting indicators - you will be able to determine whether a stock is worth trading or not.

Free bonus #3: **Amazons DCF Model Revealed ($37 value)**

This Excel spreadsheet will be a great companion for you whilst reading this book. It will reveal the complete DCF model calculations I've presented in the book for Amazon. With this insightful spreadsheet, you will find it easier to duplicate my DCF model example on any company you're researching.

Free bonus #4: Colored Images – Fundamental Analysis for Beginners

To keep our books at a reasonable price for you, we print in black & white. But here are all the images in full color.

All of these bonuses are 100% free, with no strings attached. You don't need to provide any personal details except your email address.

To get your bonuses, go to the link or QR code:

www.az-penn.com

A.Z Penn

Glossary

10K - the annual report filing with the SEC.

10Q - the quarterly report filing with the SEC.

Accounts payable - amounts the company owes to its suppliers who haven't been paid at the balance sheet date.

Accounts receivable - amounts that customers owe to the company and haven't paid at the balance sheet date.

Accrual - the method of accounting which aims to 'match' costs and income with the period which they cover and which is used in the income statement. It's different from cash accounting, which shows transactions when the money is actually paid over.

Acid test - cash and accounts receivable divided by current liabilities. It's a measure of the company's ability to meet a short term cash crunch and to pay its bills as they come due.

Amortization - writing off the cost of an intangible asset such as software or goodwill over its expected useful life.

Annual report - every company has to issue an annual report giving details of its financial situation. Companies listed on a stock exchange also have to give other details.

Asset allocation - an approach to investment which looks at how an investor's portfolio should be divided between different types of assets.

Asset - something owned by a company, such as cash, plant, or real estate. It also includes amounts owed to the company by customers, which should eventually be turned into cash.

Balance sheet - the statement of what the company owns (assets) and owes (liabilities).

Beta - a quantification of a share's volatility - that is, how much its price moves compared to a given move in the market.

Bond - a security issued by a company, entitling the bondholder to a payment of interest ('coupon').

Book value - the value of a company's assets as shown on the balance sheet. This is based on the purchase cost, so it may not represent what they are actually worth if put up for sale.

CAGR - Compound Average Growth Rate: a way of measuring long term growth averages.

Capital asset - an asset employed long term in the business, such as a data server, paper-making plant, or airplane.

Capital expenditure - money spent on capital assets.

Cash flow - the cash that the company has received and paid out over the year, shown in the cash flow statement. This is different from the income statement, which shows profit on an accrual basis.

Confirmation - this is one of the rules in Dow Theory - trends must always be confirmed by another indicator or trend. As a fundamental analyst, you should also expect management's discussion of operations to be confirmed by the numbers you see in the report.

Consolidated statement - this statement consolidates (puts together) all the company's subsidiary companies to arrive at a view of the finances of the whole organization.

Constant dividend model - see Gordon Growth Model.

Contingent liability - a liability which could crystallize, but has not done so. For instance, a lawsuit *might* be lost, and if the company can estimate roughly how much that would cost, it will record this in the notes to the accounts. But since the company could still win the lawsuit, it is not fair to record the liability in the balance sheet.

Contrarian - an investor who aims to make money by taking a view that opposes the market trend.

Cost of goods sold (COGS) - the direct cost of a product or service. For a retailer, it will be the cost at which goods are bought in; for a manufacturer, the cost of the materials and components used in a product, and any other costs which can be *directly* tied to the product. It excludes marketing, sales and other overhead costs.

Current asset - an asset that is expected to be turned into cash in the short term, such as inventories or accounts receivable, and including cash and short term liquid investments such as bonds or treasury bills.

Current liability - a liability that needs to be paid in the short term, such as amounts owing to suppliers and short term debt.

Current ratio - current assets divided by current liabilities. It's a measure of the company's ability to pay its bills as they come due, but it's not as stringent as the acid test.

Debt - any money the company has borrowed, and on which it has to pay interest (or which it has to redeem at a premium).

Debt/equity ratio - debt as a percentage of equity. This shows the relationship between the two sources of funding and can indicate whether the company is running a high financial risk.

Deferred assets - a deferred asset is something that has already been paid for but hasn't been used. For instance, if a company buys its insurance in November and has a December year-end, 11 months of the annual premium will be treated as a deferred asset.

Deferred income - when a customer pays in advance, and the company hasn't yet earned the income (by providing the service or product), the amount is treated as deferred income. Companies which rent or provide subscription services will have relatively large amounts of deferred income.

Depreciation - the writing down of the cost of a tangible (physical) asset over its useful life as part of the accruals method of accounting.

Diluted net income per share - net income divided by shares in issue *plus* shares that have not yet been issued but are to be issued in the future (e.g. those relating to employee stock option schemes).

Discounted Cash Flow (DCF) - a method of valuing a company by discounting future cash flow to today's value.

Diversification - reducing risk by spreading your asset allocation between different asset classes or between different stocks and sectors.

Dividend - the amount paid by a company to its shareholders out of net income for the year. Not all companies pay a dividend.

DRIP - a dividend reinvestment scheme. Many companies offer a scheme by which shareholders can choose to receive their dividend in shares instead of cash. If the DRIP has zero brokerage fees, it may be to your advantage to choose the shares.

Dow Theory - a set of theories evolved by Charles Dow which is at the heart of technical analysis and which looks at trends in market prices and their likelihood of continuation.

Earnings announcement - stock exchange listed companies are required to announce their earnings on a regular basis. For NYSE and Nasdaq stocks, they must release quarterly figures through the SEC's EDGAR system.

Earnings per share (net income per share) - that proportion of income after tax which relates to each share; total net income divided by the number of shares in issue.

Earnings yield - the inverse of the P/E ratio: enables comparison between the company's valuation and other forms of return such as WACC or bond yields.

EBIT - operating earnings before interest and tax: a good level to judge the performance of the business operations of the company before looking at its financing.

EBITDA - earnings before interest, tax, depreciation, and amortization: EBIT with the depreciation charge shown in the cash flow statement added back to show an approximation of operating cash flow (since depreciation is not a cash item).

EDGAR - The Electronic Data Gathering Analysis and Retrieval System of the SEC, which handles company reports, including earnings announcements.

Equity - the owner's / shareholders' capital in a business. Unlike debt, it is permanent capital that does not have to be repaid.

Exchange-traded fund (ETF) - a fund, usually copying a stock exchange index and with low costs, that can be bought and sold on the stock exchange.

FINRA - the Financial Industry Regulatory Authority, which regulates brokers and exchanges in the USA.

GAAP - generally accepted accounting principles that guide auditors in compiling a company's accounts.

Gordon Growth Model - a way to find the present value of a continued stream of regular payments at a steady growth rate. Also known as the Constant Dividend Model.

Gross margin - gross profit as a percentage of sales. A key ratio for retailers.

Gross profit - sales revenue less cost of goods sold (COGS).

Income statement (or profit and loss account) - the financial statement which shows the company's revenues, costs and profit for the period, using the accruals method of accounting.

Intangible assets - assets which are not physical; for instance, intellectual property, copyrights, and goodwill in acquired businesses.

Inventory turnover (stock turnover) - cost of sales divided by the average value of inventory.

Liquidity risk - the risk of being unable to sell an asset (e.g. a stock, inventory, or real estate) in order to realize cash proceeds: the risk of being unable to pay short term debts because of the inability to realize those assets.

Long term assets (Fixed assets) - assets that are intended for use in the business over the long term.

Long term liabilities - liabilities which do not have to be repaid within the next year, including long term borrowings.

Management discussion and analysis of operations - the portion of the annual report in which management explains the industry conditions, operations of the company, and financial results. "The words to go with the numbers."

Margin - any profit figure as a percentage of sales revenues.

Market capitalization - the total value of a company's shares at the market price (the share price times the number of shares in issue).

Market risk - see system risk.

Moving average - a chart line showing the average of the stock price over a certain period, smoothing out the 'noise' of day-to-day price movements.

Multiple - see P/E ratio.

NASDAQ - one of the USA's two major stock exchanges. The other is NYSE.

Net income/profit/loss - what is left of the profits once the company has paid its debt servicing and taxes. This is the profit that 'belongs' to shareholders and out of which dividends are paid.

Net worth - the sum total of the shareholders' equity, which is equal to the company's assets less its borrowings and other non-equity liabilities.

Non-recurring items - income or expenses which are not expected to happen again, for instance, the sale of a major property, a restructuring charge, or a large legal settlement.

NYSE - the New York Stock Exchange, one of the USA's two major exchanges.

Off-balance-sheet liability - liabilities which are not shown on the balance sheet, either because they are not yet certain (e.g. a lawsuit still in progress) or because they have been put in a non-recourse special vehicle company (SPV). The latter are now much more difficult to hide.

Operating profit/loss - see EBIT.

P/E ratio - the share price divided by net income per share. A measure of valuation - how many years the company will take to 'earn' its share price.

Price to book - the share price compared to net assets per share.

Primary market - the market in which companies issue new shares for money which goes to the company itself.

POC - percentage of completion, a method of accounting for large contracts such as civil engineering works.

Pre-tax profit - profit after interest payment but before tax. It is regarded as the main figure in the UK, but in the US, analysts focus on EBIT and net income.

Provision - an entry in the balance sheet to reflect a probable, quantified risk, such as bad debts (e.g. bank customers who cannot repay their borrowings).

Ratio - a quantitative relation between two figures; a way of comparing two numbers to each other (e.g. price to sales, EBIT to sales, net income to assets).

Resistance level - in technical analysis, a share price level beyond which the share price does not rise and which 'resists' upward movement.

Retained earnings - net income once the dividend has been paid, which is kept on the balance sheet as part of shareholders' equity. It is available for investment or for paying dividends in future years.

ROA (Return on Assets) - net income as a percentage of average assets: a measure of the company's ability to use its assets to generate profit.

ROE (Return on Equity) - net income as a percentage of shareholders' equity: a measure of the efficiency of the company's capital structure as well as its use of physical assets to generate profit.

Revenues - income generated by sales of goods or services or through rentals.

Risk tolerance, risk aversion, risk appetite - are ways of describing the amount of risk an investor is prepared to run. This will depend partly on the investor's financial situation and other circumstances and partly on personal preference.

SEC - the Securities and Exchange Commission, a government agency which polices the U.S stock markets.

Secondary market - the stock market, in which existing shares are traded between investors. The money in secondary market transactions does not go to the company but to the seller of the shares.

Specific risk - the risk that is specific to an individual asset or company and that is not shared with other types of assets or other companies. This risk can be mitigated by diversification.

Spread: 1. the difference between the price at which a stock is bought and that at which it is sold by specialists; 2. the difference between a bond yield and the yield on the market or 10 year Treasuries.

Support level - in technical analysis, the opposite of a resistance level; a share price that acts as the bottom of the trading range and below which the price does not fall.

System risk - the risk of the market as a whole. You cannot diversify away from this risk.

Tangible assets - physical assets such as stock, buildings, or vehicles.

Technical analysis - looking at patterns of share price behavior to predict likely outcomes: 'charting'.

Terminal value - the expected value of a business at the end of the period used in discounted cash flow calculations.

Trading range - in technical analysis, the high and low price levels between which a share price tends to fluctuate.

Trend - the direction in which revenues, margins, and share prices tend to move.

Volatility - the likelihood of a stock price to move by more (or less) than the movement of the market as a whole.

WACC - Weighted Average Cost of Capital: the amount the company has to pay for its debt (i.e. the interest rate on each of its loans) and equity.

Working capital - inventory and accounts receivable less accounts payable.

Write-off, write-down - reducing the value of an asset which has become less viable, such as a debt that is unlikely to be paid or shares held which are worth less than their purchase price.

Yield (dividend yield) - the dividend paid as a percentage of the share price.

A.Z Penn

Endnote, for those who made it this far.

The *wrong* answer to how to check economic and company data was 'ordering the most expensive drink you can at Starbucks'. If you want to know, it cost $47.30 and is a Quadraginoctuple Frap: and if you want to watch it being ordered and made, you can look at:

www.youtube.com/watch?v=s0puNRBLH7s

Or search on YouTube: **($47.30) World's Most Expensive Starbucks Drink - "Quadriginoctuple Frap"**

Fundamental Analysis for Beginners

Quiz Answers

Chapter 1:
1. d
2. c
3. c
4. a
5. c

Chapter 2:
1. c
2. a
3. d
4. c
5. b

Chapter 3:
1. c
2. a
3. c
4. c
5. b

Chapter 4:
1. c
2. c
3. a
4. c
5. b

Chapter 5:
1. c
2. c
3. a
4. a
5. b

Chapter 6:
1. b
2. b
3. c
4. b
5. c

Chapter 7:
1. b
2. b
3. d
4. a
5. d

Chapter 8:
1. b
2. c
3. d
4. a
5. d

Chapter 9:
1. c
2. b
3. a
4. a
5. d

Chapter 10:
1. a
2. a
3. d
4. b
5. c

Chapter 11:
1. d
2. c
3. c
4. d
5. d

Chapter 12:
1. b
2. b
3. a
4. c
5. a

Chapter 14:
1. b
2. b
3. d
4. c
5. a

Fundamental Analysis for Beginners

270